The Story of a Dreamer

Anilu Castro

WRITERS REPUBLIC L.L.C.
515 Summit Ave. Unit R1
Union City, NJ 07087, USA

Website: *www.writersrepublic.com*
Hotline: *1-877-656-6838*
Email: *info@writersrepublic.com*

Ordering Information:
Quantity sales. Special discounts are available on quantity purchases by corporations, associations, and others. For details, contact the publisher at the address above.

Library of Congress Control Number:		2019951381	
ISBN-13:	978-1-64620-025-2	[Paperback Edition]
	978-1-64620-026-9	[Hardback Edition]
	978-1-64620-027-6	[Digital Edition]

Rev. date: 09/20/2019

To all Dreamers

Acknowledgements

I want to thank God firstly for the many miracles He has made in my life. I am nothing without Him and I am grateful for all blessings and trials He has sent upon me. All my appreciation to my mother Ana, my father Manuel and my sister Violeta for standing by my side all my life. I am so thankful for your love, support and moments spent together. Life would suck without any of you!

My infinite appreciation to Geovanna Paco Montesinos for all the input and support throughout this project. This book would have not been finished if I hadn't met you! You are a great friend and an even better representative of my LDS family! I love you!

A special thanks to my adoptive auntie Martha Mauss, Joe Simonds aka "Pepe the Jefe", my fake brother Nam Nguyen, my leaders Kevin Ehringer, Mike Cox, Jan Thevenet and the rest of my DCS family for the many opportunities, encouragement, confidence and many, many laughs. I love you all to the moon and back, and I am one lucky girl for getting to work with all of you, amazing people! This place would not be the same without the pure love and efforts of each member.

I can't thank my friends enough for all the motivation and support they had given me throughout these years. Shout out to Erika Barron, Elizabeth Martinez, Vasti Fasanelli, Eduardo Bonilla, Ariel Fasanelli, Leticia Fraga, Andrea Escobar, Jose "Pepe Revoltoso" Lazaro Mendez, Francisca Rodriguez and my editor Linda Tucker for being such great guides and mentors, regardless of the distance. Each one of you is a great example of what type of human beings the world needs more of. I wouldn't have made it this far without each one of you!

Lastly, I want to tell all those people whom once harmed me, that I do not hold any regrets or hate against you. I forgive and thank you for the suffering brought because without y'all, this story would have never been written.

"These Dreamers are Americans in their hearts, in their minds, in every single way but one: in paper. They were brought to this country by their parents, sometimes even as infants. They may not know a country besides ours. They may not even know a language besides English. They often have no idea they are undocumented until they apply for a job, or college, or a driver's license." – Barack Obama

Introduction

When my dad's mother died, she asked my dad to take care of her children since he was the most mature. My dad, Manuel, promised her he was going to satisfy her last wish and he did. He raised his six brothers and three sisters.

When he was fifteen years old, he started working in Mexico City. He worked during the night and went to school in the mornings. People who knew him said he was very smart. At school, he was one of the best students, always having high grades.

By the time his younger brother Gustavo, was halfway done with high school, he began to realize what he really wanted to do. He told my dad he wanted to go to college and finish a professional career. My father felt so glad to know he wanted to create a better future for himself. With his hand crossing his heart, he swore Gustavo he will help him become the best lawyer of Mexico City.

When my father was just a few months away from graduating, some students set the classroom up to fire forcing him to drop out of school. He then started working full time at an aluminum company after the incident. He worked hard every day to be able to pay my uncle's classes; which were very expensive.

One day while riding the train back from school, Gustavo was assaulted by three young guys. The robbers had taken all his books, the few bills he had in his wallet and even the old shoes he was wearing. Very concerned about the situation, my father promised him it will never happen again. With the following check he received, my father replaced the books Gustavo needed to continue studying. And three months after that, he bought him his first car.

Manuel, my father, had only one addiction in his life: soccer. He practiced almost every day after work. He didn't share this often, but he was very close to playing on a first-division professional team. His passion for the sport led him to make good friends. At his job, engineers, lawyers, accountants, managers, and even the president went in search of him every Friday. They all formed a soccer team and Dad was always the only employee invited to join them.

Dad never rejected an opportunity to play soccer. He was always down for helping any team. At the age of twenty-two years old, he was training with a second-division team looking forward to continuing his career as a soccer player. But a Saturday morning at a friendly game, a brutal player ended up with my father's dream breaking his leg. The injury was so terrible that left my dad in bed for more than one year. At the age of twenty-two years, the doctors prohibited him from kicking a ball for the rest of his life. There was nothing he could do to be able to play again. His dream was over. However, his brother's dream was not. After he recovered, he saw his little brother Gustavo graduate and become a lawyer in Mexico City.

Mom, on the other hand, was very similar to my dad. Their eighteen-year age difference couldn't be noticed when it came to hard work. Mom has six brothers and two sisters. She talks way more about her past than Dad does. My grandma was a very strict mother to her children. Since the day mom turned 6 years old, she made her work hard. She was the one that took care of her younger siblings. Her family was so poor that none of them got too far on their education. Mom only made it to 3rd grade of Elementary.

She tells me that grandma wouldn't let her go to school unless the house was completely clean. Her childhood was very difficult. My grandfather had problems with alcohol. He used to come home at night drunk every day; would hurt anybody that stood on his way, especially his children. Mom thought about running away from home a couple of times, but then she realized how much she loved her family. She was well trained on cooking, one of her favorite hobbies to do today. She married Dad at the age of eighteen years old, and that was how the story of a family of dreamers began.

Chapter

I

He was old and alone in that big house. Cried every day for his lovely wife who rested in peace for two years already. He was feeling sick, and most of his children didn't care. He seemed weak and skinny. There were days he wouldn't eat. His hair was white. Mom convinced Dad to move in with him. I was watching everything from Mom's belly. Since the day my parents moved with him his attitude changed. He was feeling very content. He smiled and seemed to forget about his wife's death.

Mom cooked mountains of food for him to eat. She had to change his diapers just like a baby. She and Dad gave the love he asked for, the attention none of his children gave and the care he needed. It seemed like if expiration time was coming close for him. He was getting mental problems. He wouldn't remember anything from the day before. My mom had to give him his showers while Dad bought the medications he needed to help him feel better. He loved him. Of course, it was his father; my grandpa.

In the mornings, he would get up very early and go for a walk. Sometimes he would get lost like a little kid as he tried to find his way back home. Usually, he was no more than a block away, and a friend of my parents or a neighbor would bring him home. Mom tried to keep him in the house, but he escaped anyway. He would go looking for his other kids. Sometimes, he would make it to one of his sons' houses, but when they saw him coming, they would shut their doors and windows. Just like that; they felt neither shame nor remorse.

Dad took care of grandpa's animals. He cared for them every day along with his own. Dad kept all the animals together at his farm where he spent most of the day working.

One afternoon, after about five months, Grandpa returned from one of his excursions and announced that he wanted Mom and Dad to move out. My parents were very surprised; they didn't want to leave him alone, but he insisted angrily that he didn't want them living with him anymore. Mom and Dad didn't want to argue with him, so they moved back to our old house. Even then, Mom continued to care for him. She would cook and would send one of his nephews to grandpa's house to check on him and take him some food. He accepted the food, but angrily; accepting the meals probably felt like an acknowledgment of his increasing helplessness. Mom and Dad found his attitude confusing and frustrating, but they tried hard to remember that he was old and wasn't always in control of his actions and words.

One Saturday morning, my grandpa's neighbor came running to our house. Breathlessly, he told my mom that he had found grandpa very sick. My mom was very pregnant at the time. Nonetheless, without a second thought, she headed for Grandpa's house, which was about 2 miles away. She walked as quickly as she could. She arrived to find Grandpa on the floor sweating and crying out in pain. Mom, who was sweaty and panting herself after the strenuous walk, was worried and uncertain about what to do. She knelt, awkwardly holding herself from the wall, doing her best to avoid hurting the baby she had inside her tummy. She touched grandpa's face and realized he was burning up. She could tell he was in a lot of pain. When she removed the blanket covering him, she saw his dirty diaper. Grandpa noticed her looking at his diaper and was embarrassed. He avoided having eye contact with mom.

The news of Grandpa's situation had spread quickly, and neighbors began arriving one by one offering to help. Dad's siblings were not among those who came. With the help of the neighbors, mom managed to get Grandpa off the floor. She went searched the house for medications while others wrapped a wet towel around Grandpa's head and tried to comfort him. Once Grandpa was upright, mom bathed him and cooked a hot chicken stew. A few hours later, two of his sons arrived at the house. They were calm, blissfully unaware of the chaos that had occurred earlier. By the time they arrived, Grandpa was looking and feeling better. His sons scolded him angrily, "Si tu no te cuidas solo, nadie lo va a hacer por ti. Deja de dar problemas." The old man looked at them, taken aback by their hostility after the kindness of his daughter-in-law and the neighbors. Then, he cast his eyes down, like a child who'd been admonished by his mother. My mother stared at them, furious, but held her tongue. She knew that any word that came out of her mouth would be the start of a long, futile argument.

Two minutes later, they left. Grandpa sat crying, while mom tried to soothe him. He hugged mom and begged her to move in with him again.

Mom gently reminded him he had been the one who made them leave previously. He hung his head again and confessed that Rosa, a daughter-in-law, had told him to kick them out because they wanted to kill him. "But I know you are not mean; I like how you treat me," the old man said. Once again, Mom convinced Dad to move in with grandpa.

Chapter

II

*G*randpa knew I was in mom's belly. He loved to play with my sister who was a year old by the time and me. My parents gave her lots of attention, bought her the most expensive milk, and spoiled her too much. When I was born, Mom had a C-section and stayed at her mother's house to recover. Dad stayed at grandpa's house to take care of him and came to see mom every single day.

One afternoon, a little kid knocked on grandma's door. He seemed very afraid as he explained hastily, "Arturo (grandpa) esta solo en la casa y nose que le pasa. Esta llorando," he added. Mom stood up as she heard the little boy say that. She'd had surgery only a few days earlier. It was impossible for her to walk. Using a tricycle, mom's brother took her to grandpa's house quickly. When she opened the door, she saw the old man on the floor again. But this time, he was very quiet. Dad wasn't aware of what was going on. He was working in a field that was 45 minutes away. He had asked the neighbor to keep an eye on grandpa while he was out and that was who found grandpa.

Mom looked around desperately. Her mind was blank; she had no idea what to do. Grandpa did not look good at all. She picked his head off the floor and held it on the palm of her head. She told my uncle and the neighbor to go find a doctor. They both ran in search of one.

The old man opened his eyes and recognized Mom immediately. "Que Bueno que veniste" he said trembling. Mom placed a soft pillow under his head to make him more comfortable and changed his diaper. He couldn't keep his eyes open for too long, but tears were coming down. He held Mom's hand tightly and begged her not to let him go, "Tengo miedo!" he confessed shaking.

She sat next to him, crying quietly, looking at the door, waiting for help to arrive. "No me dejes ir!" he cried once again. Mom was doing everything she could think of to help him, but it was useless. His face was pale, and he was shaking uncontrollably. There, in his beloved house; alone, he released Mom's hand, shed one last tear, and closed his eyes forever. Mom's tears flowed freely. Minutes later, my uncle and the neighbor came back with a doctor along with seven more people eager to help. They were too late. He was gone.

Three of them helped Mom stand while the others checked Grandpa's pulse to confirm that he was indeed gone to the other life. Dad arrived home to find the house full of people, and grandpa's body immobile on the floor. He hugged Mom who continued to cry wordlessly. Dad didn't say anything; he allowed his tears to fall. Everyone observed quietly. He looked around and recognized that the whole town was there, except his siblings.

All of grandpa's children were reunited at the funeral. They cried nonstop, not that it mattered now. It was too late to show him their love. He couldn't hear them say, "I love you, Dad." Neither one, Mom or Dad said anything to them. They bit their tongues and refrained from saying, "You should've told him that when he was still alive."

The day of the testament reading was one to remember. It was the beginning of an unpleasant altercation among brothers. Grandpa had a farm, animals, and a big house in which he lived alone for years. The judge read: "My farm and animals can be seen, visited, and taken care of by any of my kids. However, they can only be sold for emergency purposes. They all have rights to them but my house; is only Manuel's." Two clapped at grandpa's decision; they agreed Dad was the one who should have the house. The rest of them were very unhappy with what they heard. Those were the people that even though they had everything, they wanted more.

Dad was caught off guard. It was a total surprise for everyone in the room. He looked down to avoid his siblings' angry faces. They had their own houses, but they knew grandpa's house was worth a lot of money. After the reading, Dad called a meeting to inform everyone how grandpa had passed away and to remember him as the good person he was. Brothers, sisters, in-laws, and close friends were present at that meeting. Dad told his siblings that he did not want to own Grandpa's house by himself. "As well as the farm and animals, I want my siblings to know that the house belongs to all of us; the only condition is that the house can never be sold." His brothers became even angrier when they heard that. One stood up and accused my father of living with grandpa for his own gain. "You knew he would die soon, and you wanted to own all of his goods" he argued. Another brother, Alfonso agreed with him and accused Dad of stealing grandpa's animals.

God, grandpa, and the rest of us knew that all of that was a big lie. Dad had worked hard for everything he had. He wasn't one to obtain things easily. Even Gustavo, the brother my dad had helped become a lawyer, was against him.

Most of the people present stood up for my dad, including my aunt Lucia, whose anger increased every time her brothers said a word. She knew they were wrong and wanted to make them understand the situation. The room was in chaos. Everyone was arguing except Dad who just stood quietly until things quieted down. He starred at his brothers seriously and said: "If that is really what you think of me, I don't deserve to be your brother; I know you are more important people than I am. You went to school and thank God you are professionals. I am nobody compared to you, but something I am very sure of is that I have never stolen anything in my life, especially from my own family. You can have everything: animals, the farm, and the house. I do not want anything" he said in a broken voice. "I am just going to ask you for one last thing: don't ever call me brother again. You don't deserve to have such a thief as a sibling."

Dad walked away crying. Aunt Lucia followed him, but he asked her to leave him alone. He walked out the door and down the street until he found a quiet, dark spot. He cried all night alone and came back home when he felt ready to face the world again.

The following morning, my father gave his brothers all the animals that belonged to grandpa. He also made a copy of the key to grandpa's house and gave one to each of them. Later that year, he was informed that all of grandpa's animals had been sold.

The money was invested in parties. However, they claimed that all the money had been invested in grandpa's funeral. The farm was sold as well. The only thing left was grandpa's house which was abandoned; just like they had abandoned his tomb.

Chapter

III

*D*uring my childhood, my family struggled. It was very difficult to live in Chiapas. There were no jobs, a lot of poverty, and mean people. However, we didn't want to leave because we had our own house and Dad owned some land.

To survive, Dad worked day and night cutting grass in a field while Mom sold chips, cokes, candies, beer, and bread in a new store we had at our house. Mom made the bread herself. People loved it. She didn't get much from it, but they managed to buy what they could with what she earned.

I remember my home as if it were yesterday when I last saw it. Many people including me thought our house was the most beautiful house in the town. My father had made that house brick by brick.

Dad's intelligence and great ideas made the 1-bedroom house look like a palace. He didn't have a day off from work. During the weekends, he worked at my house building new things. He built Mom a huge oven that was made from mud on which she baked her bread. On the big patio, he planted mango, guava, lemon, and pepper trees along with colorful flowers everywhere. In between the 2 mango trees, he built a small chapel where we prayed before going to sleep.

In the middle of the patio, he built a well of water which was very deep, and tall enough to prevent kids from falling into it. The patio was so immense that even after all that, we still had a lot of room to run and play.

Besides the animals at the farm, we had pigs, chickens, and two adorable dogs living on our property. Dad didn't like to sit around and waste time. To this day, his favorite words are: "If God keeps giving me strength, I will keep working hard."

He is the kind of man who will give his life for his family without a second thought. He gave us everything. As well, he gave food to people who had nothing to eat. He opened our home to less fortunate kids and let them play with our toys. He would advise them as a father when they didn't have one. He didn't care how many of his animals got cooked if he took the hunger away from people.

He loves to nickname people, especially kids. He finds the perfect and most hilarious nicknames. As kids, we laughed when we heard other kids calling each other by their nicknames. Random kids would stand outside my house, shyly, to ask my father if he needed help on something. That's how my father knew they were hungry. They would offer to work for their food but of course; Dad didn't let them. Instead, he made them play soccer.

Right in front of my house, there was a big piece of land that was in poor condition. It was full of tall grass and nasty puddles. People say that land used to be a jungle, but no one could prove if that story were true. Dad used his off time to clear the grass from that land. On his water breaks, he sat quietly by himself outside my house and stared at the land he was clearing as if he knew already what the land was going to be used for when he finished. It took him a while, but he made the most beautiful soccer field in the town. Kids and adults benefited from Dad's labor. Our small business benefited too. My parents sold a lot of drinks when the field was used, especially beer, while kids bought chips and candies after every game.

Dad never dreamed his business would become more successful because of the soccer field. The Corona Company increased the amount of beer they distributed to our store. Unfortunately, my father made the kind of mistake that men like him make; he trusted people too much, to the point that he started selling on credit to the people in the town.

They drank until they fell asleep or couldn't stand up. The situation started to get worse to the point that he had to borrow money from other people to be able to pay the company what he owed them. This started happening a lot. Mom and Dad argued about it all the time. Then, God gave us a lesson that changed our lives drastically.

One night, while Mom and Dad argued on the patio, someone sneaked into our house and took all the money my parents had for the Corona Company that month. The next day, when the company came to get the earnings, my parents didn't have one cent to give them.

My father explained to them that we had been robbed, but they didn't believe him. They gave him one week to pay off the whole month's debt or face going to jail. In desperation, my parents tried to borrow money from people, but most were so poor that only mom's godmother was able to help them on one condition: "You cannot stay in Chiapas."

She gave them enough money to run away, but it was not even half of the debt to Corona. We only had one way out. Late at night, my father looked around our 'palace' and cried quietly. There were two bedrooms under construction, one for each of his princesses. Those were two bedrooms he never got to finish. One day before the debt had to be paid, we got into a taxi, heartbroken. Leaving behind our house, animals, farm, land, and a lot of debts, we escaped early in the morning.

Chapter

IV

ur destination was Ciudad Juarez, Chihuahua where my mom's younger sister resided with her family. There, we began a whole new life again starting from the bottom. We arrived with nothing. I was 7 years old then and going into the third grade. My aunt, Guadalupe, had a one-year-old son. We loved playing with him.

In our town, only grandma and mom's godmother knew where we were heading. However, they made everyone believe they had no idea where we were just to keep us safe.

People made up stories about our disappearance. The people from the company threatened grandma saying they would kill my father for running away with their money. But things were not the way they thought. Grandma just listened and kept her words to herself although she was suffering on the inside. Only God knew when she would next see us.

Meanwhile, in Juarez, my father was feeling desperate. He missed Chiapas. We all did. It took him a while to get used to the drastic change. He wanted to work. He paced back and forth inside the house. My aunt Guadalupe helped him get a job where she worked. It was at a huge company known worldwide: "Lear." They had over a thousand employees. The building was huge. They had an immense cafeteria and many cooks ready to prepare what they wanted to eat. The company paid for all the food consumed by their employees. There were also flat screen televisions Inside the cafeteria.

During the world cup, the whole company stopped working when Mexico's national team was playing and united in supporting "El Tri." My father loved that, of course. He soon became friends with people and loved his job. Dad's first checks were directly sent to Chiapas to pay off all his debts. He even sent extra money to those people he owed including the Corona Company. Still, some people continued to hate him, and some claimed he was not welcome in the town ever again.

Others hoped Dad would return to take their hunger away like he used to. My mother's father took care of my dad's farm and animals while our house was visited by my uncles once in a while. It was abandoned most of the time. My uncles said the house was getting web spiders everywhere.

My new school was very different from the one in Chiapas. It was much bigger, and there were much more activities. My first year was the toughest, of course. I had always been shy and quiet, which made it harder to make friends. I also had a hard time understanding my classmates. They talked differently. I didn't know I spoke a portion of a different language until my teacher told me. She explained to me that some people from the south of Mexico had a different language which was called "dialect." There were hundreds of different dialects spoken in Mexico. I believed her when I tried talking to my classmates, and they only understood half of what I was telling them.

It was frustrating trying to have even a short conversation with them when they could not understand what I was saying completely. I felt like they were playing a joke on me. I wanted to think that was the case.

My sister and I were the only people from the south in the whole school. She had the same problem as me. We sat together on a bench quietly during lunchtime and watched the boys play soccer. Not one girl played sports in that school as far as I could tell. My sister made friends and joined the boys on the soccer field. She preferred playing soccer rather than eating during lunch time.

She often went home with bruises on her legs. Every day she had a new one. Since the bruising was getting worse and worse, my parents forbade her to play soccer with the boys again. She violated my parent's rules anyway.

"I will tell our parents!" I threatened her when she walked down the field.

I made a good business deal with her. She paid me for my silence by giving me her lunch money every day. They gave us 5 Pesos each. By lunchtime, I had ten Pesos which was enough for a bean burrito and a coke. I remember walking to the field and sitting on the bench eating my burrito and my coke in front of her while she starved. It was kind of cruel, but I had a good time laughing at her.

My father bought her about ten soccer balls. Each one of them ended up on top of the school wire completely flat. But she didn't worry; she knew Dad would get her another one.

After a few months at my new school, I joined the basketball team. It was lots of fun! We competed against other schools during school hours, which was awesome. Sometimes, we were gone for a whole day if we played more than one game. My interest in the sport was unusual in my family. I was the first person to play the sport. I wasn't sure if I really enjoyed playing basketball or if I enjoyed being away from classes. It started to get boring after a while, so I quit the following year.

I then joined their choir band, which was the very first time they were doing it. The entire school got to try out to be in the band. Each audition lasted one minute, and it consisted in standing next to the teacher and sing the national anthem while he played the piano.

It was fun to see some of the auditions. Some students were nervous, others didn't even know the national anthem, and I saw a few of them start cracking up as soon as the teacher began playing the piano. There were only 10 spots in the band and over 200 students auditioned. Surprisingly, my sister and I were chosen as part of the band. I don't know what the teacher liked about us since we were both very shy and we didn't even like to sing.

The week after the auditions, the choir teacher took the 10 of us to the principal's office. The principal wanted to hear each of us sing individually. He was mean. All the students were afraid of him. It was funny to hear that not one of us got past the first line of the national anthem. It was as though we all planned to forget the lyrics. He was pissed. I can't even remember all the mean things he yelled, but he made some girls cry. As a principal, he was serious, strict, and not even a bit fun. I never saw him smile. I guess he just took his job a little too seriously.

During our first couple presentations, my sister and I had no idea what was going on in the performances. We'd usually line up at the very back of the group and had an entire conversation between us while the rest of the band kept singing. To our favor, we never got caught although we did distract some of the other kids in the band.

Chapter

V

We started building a new home after my aunt Guadalupe left us. She and her family had migrated to the United States and settled in Los Angeles, California. It was sad she was gone, but we were happy she had new opportunities. She became established in the United States and decided to change her life for good.

My aunt was the first person from mom's family to get to the United States. She called us almost every day. My dad was still working for the same company, and Mom was working with a new lady she met whose name was Hilda. Hilda lived right across the street from us. Mom did the cleaning and cooking at her house. She was kind to my family. My sister and I loved to spend time at her house which was the biggest house in the neighborhood. It had a huge pool which was the most attractive thing for us.

She taught us how to embroider cartoon faces, and we learned how to play many table games with her daughter. Her whole family was very friendly. They loved to stand in the kitchen watching Mom and admiring her delicious hand-made tortillas. They fought over each tortilla that came out of the comal. Mom smiled; she would have spent the whole day in the kitchen if that's what it took to make them happy.

Towards the end of 1999, we had moved to a house that was right next to Hilda's house. Compared to our previous house, our new house was way more peaceful and beautiful. It was kind of hidden and had two patios, one of them was full of trees. The owner was an elderly lady named Tomasita. She lived across the patio with her only daughter, Leticia.

She and Hilda seemed like two angels sent from heaven. I wish the world were full of people like them. Leticia worked in El Paso, Texas and she drove about one hour every day to get there. Tomasita stayed home all day by herself.

Every day after school, my sister and I went to her house and helped her do dishes, wash the floor, do laundry or just chill with her until her daughter came back. Tomasita and Leticia loved us as much as we loved them. Leticia tried to give us money many times to pay for the time we spent with her mom. When we would not accept it, she brought us something from El Paso each week. We were the happiest girls in the world.

We got dolls, candies, clothes, shoes, hair accessories, and table games to name a few. My parents were embarrassed by how much money she spent on us, but she always told them: "Your girls deserved more than this!"

While we were living in that house, three of my mom's brothers came to visit us from Chiapas. They planned to stay with us for two weeks and then go back but changed their minds the first week they arrived there. One of our neighbors offered them a job, and they liked the idea. Mom and Dad welcomed them to stay if they wanted, so they did.

After a few days, they met Hilda and her family as well as Leticia and Tomasita. To everyone's surprise, Leticia fell in love with my youngest uncle, Antonio, right away. Tony, as we call him, was very shy. He smiled and look down whenever Leticia looked at him. Leticia was about 30 years old and a very serious person. Even though everyone in my family loved Leticia to death, my uncle Antonio had no interest in building a relationship with her. He was too young and still a teenager. He didn't feel ready. When Leticia gave up on having a relationship, they became good friends.

My uncles worked at a company that seemed to me to be the best job in the world. They worked packing gummy worms, which were one of my favorite candies. The refrigerator always had a permanent spot for gummy worms, and Mom hid them when she noticed I was having too many. I always found them though. They worked for that company for about 6 months. Then work got so slow that they had to lay off a lot of people including my uncles. They did not enjoy staying home. They liked to work and make money, but it was getting harder and harder to find a job. They felt hopeless but didn't want to go back to Chiapas. They liked life in Juarez where they could make more money than they made back home.

Chapter

VI

The beginning of 2000 wasn't a good time in our lives. It started with a phone call from Dad's job. Mom knew right away that could not be good. Dad hardly ever called from work. The supervisor informed Mom that Dad had had an accident. It wasn't too bad, but he was bleeding, and they wanted to send him home to get some rest.

Hilda's family drove Mom straight to Dad's job. When they got there, they noticed Dad sitting in a corner with about seven people trying to help. His right leg was resting on top of a chair while people tried to clean the blood off his injury. As the supervisor said, the injury was not big, but it didn't stop bleeding. It was hard to tell from Dad's expression how much he was hurting. Mom took him home, and he said he was feeling normal. She wrapped a big white bandage around his leg and put him to bed. He was very quiet. Something was going on in his mind for sure. Only God and he knew exactly the pain he felt.

The following day, he woke up and got ready to return to work. He told Mom he was feeling good, so he took the bus and headed to his job. Things didn't go the way he wanted. Two hours later, the supervisor called Mom once again. The injury looked worse this time. The bandage Mom had wrapped around his leg was stuck to the injury, and when they tried to remove it, part of his skin came off with it too. It was just the second day, and the injury was already the size of a penny. Everyone was worried now. Seeing Dad in silence worried us even more.

We didn't know how to help him when he was not cooperating. The injury had stopped bleeding, but there was a lot of pus coming out of it. Mom looked at my uncles trying to get suggestions for what to do. Hilda suggested taking him to the hospital, but Dad refused to go. It was very hard to help him when he was against any of their ideas.

The third day, he didn't even refuse to stay home. As usual, he woke up early and stayed in bed. He was not getting a bit better. This time the injury was not only bigger, but it was getting deeper. He was starting to moan slowly and quietly. The pus didn't stop coming out, and he had no protection around it. Mom was afraid that having a bandage around his injury would cause it to be bigger when she took it off.

On Saturday morning of that same week, Dad's pain levels reached their peak. He wouldn't let anyone, but Mom come close to him. He expressed his pain when Mom touched his injury to clean it. She came back in tears every time. She was the only one that saw how much deeper and bigger the injury was getting day by day, and she suffered along with Dad. When Mom's frustration reached its level, she let everyone willing to help in Dad's room.

They all wanted to take him to the hospital. Dad looked at Mom very bothered, I knew exactly what was going through his mind: "How are we going to pay the bill to the hospital?" She knew we didn't have one cent in savings, but she was willing to take the first step to help him. My uncles, Hilda; her husband Ramon, and Leticia were there to help. He kept refusing. "No necesito ir al hospital, estoy bien" he would say. Everyone ignored his words and took him to the car.

Mom walked behind him crying quietly as my sister, and I cried harder. We didn't know exactly what was going on. All we knew was that Daddy was sick. Now I think back and realize how strong Mom was in that situation.

The first day at the hospital was long. The doctors took Dad to a room where nobody else was allowed. We waited in the waiting room impatiently walking up and down the hallway. Handing Mom a few prescriptions, the doctor told her that Dad was fine and all he needed was rest.

His diagnosis was way too simple. There was no way Dad could be okay, but that was all we really wanted to hear.

Once in the house Dad started getting worse and worse. His pain increased every time, and he developed a fever. Mom ran around the house frantically trying anything she could think of to heal Dad. He moaned a lot. My sister and I watched her from the corner of our bed very scared. My uncles were very worried but didn't know how to help either. Mom's expression was enough to scare anyone who even attempted to get in her way.

Hilda came home that night to give Dad a shot while Letty sat next to Mom trying to get information about Dad's siblings. Mom told her everything that had happened in the past. Letty suggested calling Dad's brothers to tell them what was going on.

"People change!" she told Mom.

"There is no way a human being can refuse to see their family if they are this sick!" she insisted.

The third week after the accident things got out of control. My poor father let out his pain the whole day across the house. "Llevenme a morir a mi pueblo!" he would yell. We all cried nonstop when we were away from him. Mom was out of courage. It seemed as if all she had done to help him was for naught. Letty sat with Mom on the floor encouraging her while Dad's screams grew louder and louder.

Chapter

VII

*D*ealing with Dad's attitude was an everyday issue. How could people help him if he didn't let them touch him in the first place? Mom put some thought on what Letty had suggested about calling Dad's siblings and when she felt it was time, she finally reached out to them.

The first one she called was my aunt, Lucia who was the closest sibling to my father. Her reaction was instantaneous; she ended up fainted on the floor after hearing the news. Mom cried nonstop as my aunt's daughter picked up the phone after her to inform Mom what was going on. The last thing Mom wanted was to get another member of the family sick.

It was just the first call, and things were already worse than before. My aunt's husband told my mother he would let their other siblings know. It was then that Mom decided to call another sibling personally. It was Gustavo, the brother my dad helped become a lawyer. His ambition and money had completely changed him. He dimmed our last hope with words that are stamped on my brain: "I don't know what the hell he is doing over there. Bring him here, I'll rent him a room for a few weeks while he dies!"

Our souls were devastated. "Llevenme a morir a mi pueblo!" was the only thing that came out of Dad's lips. Mom was thinking seriously of taking him back to Chiapas. We didn't know if he would recover and she was giving up.

The following morning Hilda and Letty came home determined to figure out what was going on with his injury. They took him to a different hospital to be observed and tested. The doctors diagnosed that my father had severe diabetes. In other words, they would have to cut Dad's leg off if we wanted to keep him alive.

We could not even imagine seeing Dad without one leg, and I was sure he would prefer death to that. Mom cried nonstop as the doctor talked. She wasn't ready for this. Walking down the emptiest hallway, she sat on the floor and kept crying. She felt useless; destroyed.

Dad was going to have to live the rest of his life in a wheelchair, and there was nothing she could do to avoid it. She blamed herself for it, she kept saying it was all her fault for not taking care of him enough. As Hilda talked to Mom, a young man approached Mom out of nowhere and said: "what your husband has on his leg is poison!" Mom and Hilda looked at him very confused and kept listening. "Do you know how to kill poison?" he continued "with more poison!" he said stretching Mom his hand.

Mom and Hilda looked at him very confused. He grabbed Mom and walked slowly down the hallway. "No tengas miedo, quiero ayudarte" he told Mom in a soft voice and with eye contact. Mom stopped crying. At the very end of the hallway, he opened the only door that didn't describe what kind of room it was. "Come in, I will show you the cure for your husband!" he said very confidently.

The room had shelves everywhere. On the shelves, were containers full of different types of plants, powder, liquids, and branches that not even Mom recognized. Using a ladder, he reached one of the containers on the top shelf and pulled a jar full of mini Ziploc bags.

The bags contained a purple powder. It had so little that you could hardly see the powder.

"This is poison," he started.

"You are going to dissolve this powder into a full bucket of water. When the water turns completely purple, let your husband put his leg inside the bucket for one hour."

Mom and Hilda looked at each other ashamed. They didn't know what to think about him. Was he really a good person? Or was he just trying to kill people?

"What is your name?" Mom started interrogating.

"Where do you get all this stuff from?" Hilda continued.

"Why are you helping us?" both asked.

"My name is Angel," he said. "I make all these 'medications' myself. And I want to help you because you need my help!".

"Did you just say you make all these yourself?!" Hilda repeated confused.

"I was abandoned by my parents when I was a baby. One lady; who I called "Mom" picked me up and raised me. We only had each other in this world. When I was 10 years old, she was diagnosed with cancer. She needed lots of medications, hospital care, and chemo. But we barely had enough to eat every day. I was left alone a couple of months later. Since she passed away, I promised her and myself that I would work hard to become a researcher and find the cure to that horrible disease that took her away from me. Due to low resources, I couldn't go to school, but I didn't break my promise either. I started making medications myself, and my reward is to see people overcome their diseases and weaknesses. All the things you see here, come from nature; either plants or animals".

His words were becoming more and more senseless. How did he know what to mix to make medicine if he hadn't gone to school? And why was he so sure that his medication would heal Dad? His story was hard to believe, but if he had made it up, he had done a really good job because it was very touching. He noticed as Mom and Hilda stared at him very incredulously.

"Take it!" he said closing Mom's fist. "I am sure you will come back and ask me for some more!"

Mom and Hilda walked out of the room with nothing to say. But one thing was for sure: he had stopped Mom's tears and was able to give her hope.

Chapter

VIII

*O*n the way back home, nobody said a word. I noticed Dad making gestures indicating he was in pain; his leg was hurting, but he was too embarrassed to cry out his pain in front of Hilda and her husband. Mom and Hilda were very distracted looking out the window, Ramon very focused on the steering wheel and my sister had fallen asleep.

When we got home, Dad thanked Hilda and Ramon for their help and headed straight to his bedroom. The following day, as had become usual, he woke up in great pain. He punched the brick wall next to his bed desperately, trying to find a way to decrease his pain. Everything he did was useless. The pain was still there coming stronger every time.

"I will not rest in peace if you don't take me back to my hometown to die!" he warned Mom angrily.

She had a tray on which were the things needed to clean his injury that day; as soon as she got close to him, he slapped the tray making Mom drop it. His desperation and pain were making him lose his mind. He didn't seem to understand that it was not Mom's fault that he couldn't get up from bed.

Mom was suffering as much as he was. She ran to the living room crying asking us to leave her alone for a while. It was then that she started pondering the powder she had obtained from the guy in the hospital. She felt terrified by it; what if the powder made Dad's leg worse? What if the guy was just trying to kill people? I put myself in Mom's shoes today and understand exactly how she must have felt. I remember hearing her cry silently inside the bathroom praying to God, the only one that could help her get through all this.

The following day, she woke up early in the morning. She seemed very strange. As she walked slowly to the table and sat alone to drink coffee, I saw she had in her hands, a small bag of powder. She stared at it for a long, long time pretending not to hear Dad's moaning.

She began praying on her spot, and when she got up, she looked resolved to act. Taking him a hot stew and slices of apple, she entered the room wide awake. She calmed him down saying he was scaring my sister and me every time he screamed. She sat next to him while he ate. Very slowly, she started stretching Dad's leg, giving him a careful, soft massage. She smiled at him nervously trying to recover his confidence.

He had let Mom massage his leg without saying a word. The wound was bleeding just a little but hurting a lot. After finishing his food, she grabbed the dirty dishes and took them to the sink. When she came back with him, she had the powder in her hands. She made us believe that the doctor had given it to her. She repeated the procedures to Dad as the young man had explained to her. Believing her, Dad finally got up from bed and with my uncles help, he walked to the hallway to do what he was told.

Mom ran to the restroom, got a white bucket, and filled it up with warm water. Still hesitating, she opened one of the packets and poured the powder into the water. We watched amazed as the water turned a dark, purple color.

"This must be a strong medication!" one of my uncles commented innocently.

"Stay here with your dad and don't let him take his leg off the bucket for one hour," my mom instructed me as she walked hurriedly to the restroom.

I can't imagine all that was going through Mom's head right at that moment; she knew she could be killing Dad with that powder in that instant. She took about an hour to get to the bedroom with Dad. She was just in time to help Dad get his leg out the water. Her eyes were red and swollen. I could tell she had been crying. We didn't bother to ask why.

The next morning, my sister and I woke up and walked to my parents' bedroom to have an early breakfast. My sister and I walked on one side of the bed each. Mom woke up as my sister kissed her cheeks and got up instantly to look at my dad's leg. The injury was not bleeding anymore, but there was something very weird and different that got our attention: his right calf had turned black. My mother looked very scared at his injury as my sister kept trying to wake him up. I kissed his left cheek as my sister did the same thing on his right. He didn't move.

We started tickling his stomach slowly. He seemed not to be feeling a thing. My little heart started pounding quickly as I saw a tear fall from Mom's eye as she looked at him. My sister looked very confused, not wanting to believe what Mom was thinking. I laid my ear on his chest trying to listen to his heart, but I was so nervous and scared that I heard my own heartbeat.

I shook his arm trying to get a reaction from him of some sort. Mom sat crying.

"Papa?" my sister called.

He couldn't hear us. We stood there still staring at him. It was the longest twenty seconds of my life when he suddenly jumped wide awake hugging us.

Dad had awakened that morning as a completely different person. That was the first time I saw him smile again in a long time. It was just amazing to see him change so much from one day to the next and the best thing was: he didn't complain about any pain at all.

He seemed to have forgotten about the injury he had in his right calf. Whatever the young man put in the powder was healing him. Mom continued to use the poison day by day; it was apparently, the only cure for him. She visited Angel regularly for more powder and let him know he had saved Dad's life in every chance she had. Mysteriously, Angel disappeared when Dad's leg was completely closed, and he was able to walk again.

We have no doubt he was a real angel sent from the Lord to help Dad live. We never saw him again, he had come to us to do what the Lord had commanded, and let my father live.

Today, my dad's leg is still dark from that powder. The color never faded away. We are happy it didn't because it reminds us about the many things God helped us overcome. We are reminded that the Lord gave us a second chance, and He has a purpose for my father and the whole family. And he also showed us who our real friends and family were throughout those hard times.

Chapter

IX

ad overcame many tests in life. Half of his hope and heart had been defeated in a main way. He couldn't avoid lamenting the loss of everything he owned one day. He couldn't watch a field or animals without feeling bad about losing his own. He was living in the past, thinking about the "what if's" all the time.

He said his brother turned his back on him when he needed him the most because "He is right. I deserve it!" He would say, "I am a loser." No one could make him understand he was wrong. He had failed in many ways, at least that was what he thought.

One day during a phone call with my aunt Guadalupe, Mom commented on the way my dad was acting. "He is very unhappy here," she said. Trying to help, my aunt suggested Mom to immigrate to the United States. "Get your Visa fixed and come try something new in this country" she suggested. She insisted for a long time and talked so well about living in the US that she soon convinced Mom.

However, attempting to talk to Dad about it was not easy. There was an argument every time Mom mentioned the idea. "Solo nos traera mas problemas!" he would say. His attitude was worse every time. He seemed annoyed by everyone and everything. Mom and Dad couldn't talk without ending up in a big argument that left them living like enemies for long periods.

They went to bed very mad at each other, and the following day when they woke up, they acted like enemies again. It was annoying and frustrating seeing them argue about the same thing repeatedly. Mom couldn't make Dad do what she wanted to do. It was a big decision, and she was pushing him too much. However, Dad was acting very cowardly. He didn't like trying anything new.

THE STORY OF A DREAMER

Since the day we had moved from Chiapas he didn't think about what else he could do to succeed in life. Anything different from his everyday tasks troubled him. The idea of immigrating to the US soon got to my uncles' ears, who were already dreaming about the positive change that might mean. They were young, single, and strong. Nothing was holding them back from moving forward. They began investigating. They didn't have the money needed to fix their Visa, but they found a coyote that was going to charge very little.

The coyote was recommended by one of their friends who had used him to take one of his family members to the US before. The conversation between the coyote and my uncles was quick and to the point. He had 5 conditions, which he repeated to every single person that he was going to take across.

1- "If immigration gets us for some reason, do not say that I am a coyote and that you guys are paying me to get you to the other side."

2-"The only one that carries a cell phone on the way is me and nobody else."

3- "Each person carries his own food and water."

4-"The payment is half on this side and half on the other side."

5- "I will not stop my trip for only 1 person."

This last one caught them off guard. In other words, he was saying whoever was left behind, was left behind and he wouldn't come back or wait. That sounded scary for sure. My uncles did not agree with that, but they were not in a position to argue.

The coyote planned the trip quickly and rushed to get started. The following week, my uncles were on their way to the United States of America. Their destination was Phoenix, Arizona. Each one of my uncles took a small backpack in which they carried important documents, food, water, an extra shirt, and pair of pants and of course, Mom wouldn't let them leave without a religious image.

They left so many things behind that they wanted to take with them, including us. I did not have a good feeling about all this. I was nervous from the moment they left my house, but I didn't want to be negative. Mom cried and prayed quietly in the corner of the living room. We didn't know exactly the way the coyotes moved, but we knew for sure that the trip was not going to be fun.

We spent hours sitting near the phone, waiting for it to ring hoping to hear that my uncles had made it to the other side safely. Minutes, hours, and days passed, and we still had no news on them. Mom and her sisters started making up stories over the phone about what could have happened to them, while grandma cried nonstop in Chiapas very worried. It was a whole week before my uncles communicated with us. They got to the United States with no food, no water, empty wallets, and lots of bruises.

"It was worth the pain!" they told Mom over the phone. "This place is amazing!"

Chapter

X

*M*om's curiosity and faith led her, with the help of Leticia, to convince Dad to process our Visa. Leticia and her mother, Tomasita, knew my dad respected them very much and made him listen to them. As my uncles had promised, they slowly started helping Mom financially and opened a bank account, so we could be able to meet the requirements needed for the Visa.

Hilda helped Mom get the documentation needed for the appointment. Mom made me and my sister practice every day by answering a certain number of questions that she assumed immigration would ask at the interview. She made sure we understood exactly what we were saying and what could happen if we messed up. Hilda and Leticia gave Mom all kinds of training and tips to prepare her for the important day from how to answer the questions to how to even look at them.

It was early February 2003, when the day of the interview arrived. The cold, sunless morning couldn't change Mom's excitement for what she had been waiting for. She was sure and positive that we would come back home that day with our passports stamped. Dad, on the other hand, was very serious and worried as always. He didn't look a bit happy or excited. As she helped us get dressed, Mom tested us for the very last time before heading on to the interview.

"What do you want your Visa for?" she asked that morning pretending to be the person interviewing us.

"We want the Visa to visit a relative that lives in the United States!" my sister and I replied, sounding annoyed for having repeated and listen to the same thing repeatedly for the last few weeks.

As we got on the bus that would take us to the immigration building, Mom happily fixed Dad's shirt, "your picture has to be perfect!" she said smiling at him. She carried with her a big folder full of documents that she checked as she was sitting on the bus. I'd seen her check that folder at least five times. She wanted to make sure she had everything we needed; she even carried documents we didn't need just in case.

The building was big and crowded. No seats were available, and our stomachs started crying as soon as we walked in the quiet waiting area. I felt like I was in a hospital or at a funeral. You could hear a pin drop. I could tell everyone there was nervous, and I didn't blame them. I was too. People didn't stop coming in. The place was too small to fit all the people wanting to come in.

1....2....3 hours passed, and we had moved only five steps forward. It seemed that our visit was going to take us the whole day. We saw so many people come through. Some left happy, and others couldn't even hold their heads up. Our tension increased as we gave a step closer each time. I was bored, tired and very hungry by 1 pm when we got to the front of the line.

There were only three people in front of us. Mom secretly reminded us what we were going to say for the very last time. We could totally tell from people's expressions who had obtained the Visa and who had been rejected. Their reactions just made us more nervous and insecure.

"Siguiente" the lady on the left window called. I could hear my heart beating very fast as we walked towards her.

She looked at us seriously and said: "What do you need?"

Mom answered her with her voice cutting off: "We are here to obtain a Visa." The clerk started listing all the documents we would need. "You better have every single document. Otherwise, you will have to go to the end of the line again," she said unpleasantly.

Her attitude was making us worry. "Calm down! The worse thing that can happen is to get rejected!" I told myself. I don't know what I was more afraid of getting rejected or messing up the interview and confronting Mom when we got home. The lady studied the documents for a minute, then looked at us and back to the documents.

In no time, the magic question was asked: "What do you want your Visa for?" She said looking at my sister.

Mom jumped in and started answering.

"I asked your daughter!" the clerk interrupted rudely cutting off Mom at the first word. We all looked down to avoid making my sister feel rushed or more nervous as the lady stared at her with her eyes looking above her glasses.

"We want the Visa, so we can go visit a sick relative" my sister answered softly.

"Where does your relative live?" she continued.

"In California!" Dad answered nicely. She stared at Dad for a second and then turned her attention to the documents again. She checked the documents one by one while entering the information into the computer. My sister and I leaned against the wall as she questioned my parents. I couldn't understand the questions or why they were being asked.

She stared at the computer for a while, and there was a long pause from her as she reviewed the documents. Her silence made my parents nervous. Finally, she said, "I will be back." She quickly stood up from her desk and walked towards the back of the office, where I believe higher decisions were made. It took her a good 20 minutes to come back and say: "I have an answer for you." We all turned our attention to her instantly, waiting anxiously to what she had to say.

"I have good news and bad news" she began.

"The good news is that your background is clean and ready to go. On the other hand, your bank account does not have enough money to cover you all. There is only enough money to cover one person which in this case, will be the man of the family."

Dad's expression did not change at all, but Mom's did. She looked down at the floor. It was her way of showing she felt defeated. I could only imagine how disappointed she felt. She had been so sure we would walk out of that building with everyone's Visas in hands, and now everything was turning upside down. Very quickly, the lady at the window stamped Dad's passport and handed it back to him.

As we walked towards the exit, an elderly lady who had her whole family with her waved at us, trying to get our attention. She asked softly, "Did they give you all the Visa"? I was about to open my mouth to tell her the truth when my dad interrupted me in the middle of my first word saying: "Yes, we all obtained that stamp on every single passport!" he said faking a smile. I look at him very confused. He surprised me. In fact, he surprised all of us. It was so rare of him to lie, and this was a big one. "Good Luck!" he said still faking his smile.

When we stepped out the building, I asked my dad why he had lied to the lady, and he answered: "Honey, sometimes we come across some situations in life where lying is the best way to help people. If I'd told that lady the truth, when her chance for the interview arrived, she was going to have in mind my words of disappointment. That only makes people lose faith and become more nervous. We don't want her to get rejected too!" he explained. Dad had taught me a good lesson that day, which I put into my own words: "If you are going through hell, talk to others about heaven and the beauty of it. Don't kill other people's hopes without letting them give it a try."

Chapter

XI

ne April afternoon, as we came back from school, we noticed Leticia talking to my parents. The look on Dad's face said it had already been a long conversation. As we came in, she wrapped up the conversation and left the house. The three of them acted very strangely. They were hiding something from me, and my sister and we wanted to know what was going on.

It wasn't until two weeks after and several more reunions with Letty that my parents finally decided to talk to us. Leticia's mother, Tomasita, was very sick. We hadn't seen her in a while; Mom wouldn't let us visit her as often as before, and now we knew why. That same week, Mom took us to Letty's house to see Tomasita. She looked very skinny and weak, and she could hardly move. I overheard Leticia whisper to my mom that according to the doctors, her mother was on her last stage of life.

It tore my heart knowing this. Leticia had also confessed to Mom that Tomasita was hoping she could spend the last days of life next to her siblings who lived in a different state in Mexico. It was heartbreaking to see such a nice lady slowly starting to leave this world. I just wish people like her were immortal here on earth.

Leticia moved to Jalisco with Tomasita as soon as she could to fulfill her wish. That decision meant that we had to move as well since she had no return date. That was the last time we saw them both. Hilda, who lived next to their house, said they never came back. I never forgot about them and all the things they did for my family. If I were born again, my wish would be to meet Leticia and Tomasita again, and if I could, I would change the ending of their story to a happy one.

It was that same spring that my family was split for the very first time. After having many arguments, Mom and Dad decided that my lovely father would have to emigrate from Mexico. According to them, that was the best for everyone. They planned the whole trip too soon. To make sure Dad wouldn't change his mind, Mom and Hilda used all my family's savings to buy dad's ticket and some other things he would need to take to the other side to start a new beginning.

We had only one month left to spend with Dad until he was gone. Who knew when we'd see him next? None of us could think of a way to spend the last month with Dad happily; instead, we sat around looking at him sadly. He was not a bit excited about his trip. He was being forced to leave, but we all knew it needed to happen to go further in life.

We all wished we could go with my dad and start again together. "He will come and visit us every 2 weeks!" Mom lied to us as we sobbed loudly saying goodbye to my father the day of his departure.

Both knew that would not happen. Once Dad crossed that line, there was no turning back. I wasn't ready to continue life without a dad; I needed both parents. In fact, I didn't plan on getting used to it. The first few months after his departure was the toughest for me. I couldn't think of anything else but him. I still couldn't understand why he had to leave; I was too little to understand the situation.

I would start crying during class for no reason; told my best friend about it and it was there that I realized things could always go worse. "I never got to meet my father," he told me one day while he listened to me attentively. His reddish eyes betrayed him while he tried to be strong narrating his story to me. My mind was busy after I listened to him. I couldn't stop thinking about him and the tough childhood he had had.

"What about the kids that are abandoned when they are very little?" he asked trying to uplift me.

"Or what about the kids that were born with no father at all?"

"You are lucky, your father loves you, and sooner or later, you will be reunited with him again!" His calmness and peacefulness made me feel so much better. I enjoyed talking to him. He was very mature, even though he was only 9 years old. Kids like him were very hard to find in school, and I was one lucky girl to be both his classmate and his best friend.

Chapter

XII

y father's destination was Dallas, Texas. With the help of friends and the few family members he had in the area, he found a place to stay. The drastic change had affected him the same way it had affected us. It was hard for him to adapt to a 'new world' where he didn't know the language, traditions, people, or laws.

By his second week in the U.S., he got his first job as a construction worker where they worked from moon to moon. His first day was awful. After working hard for the whole day, Dad had asked one of his new coworkers if he could give him a ride home. But Dad forgot a small, important detail: his address. Very embarrassed, and afraid to tell the man the truth, Dad told the good man to go straight since he didn't know the name of the street, the apartments, or the city.

He was more worried about what they would say than about what would happen to him. After riding for several blocks, he told the man to drop him off at the next light. "This looks familiar," he thought. He got out of the car at that light without knowing if he should go left or right and walked for 5 hours.

The following day he woke up, got ready for his second day of work, and realized he didn't know how to get there. He told Mom as they spoke on the phone how useless he felt. Still, no matter how down he was feeling, he went out there every day to look for a job. He didn't care how hard the job was. He was willing to do anything. As he took a break from walking the entire day, he went into an ice cream shop and bought a bottle of water. There, he started a conversation with the cashier. She told him that they were looking for a popsicle vendor. My dad didn't let the opportunity pass him by. He grabbed the small notebook he had with him and drew a picture of how he had got there.

He went back to his place happy that night, excited that he had found a job. But his destiny was to keep suffering for a little bit more. How much he earned was based on how much he sold per day. He walked a very long distance the whole day in unfavorable weather, hungry the entire time, and sold only five popsicles.

Dad has had many different "professions" in life. He is the most hard-working man and my greatest example. He was never afraid or embarrassed about working; it didn't matter what type of job he had been called to do.

During that time, he was very depressed. He was done with the United States; it was not the type of life he was expecting. He was ready to get his backpack and return to his country, but he had in mind his two daughters and his wife who were counting on him.

He had promised three people that he would bring them to the other side with him. So, he went out every morning full of hope and faith that he would find a job. Every single place he asked about work told him he needed paperwork to be able to get the job. "It's not like the papers are the ones that are going to work; it's me the one that will be doing the labor!" he would tell Mom desperately over the phone.

Mom encouraged him by saying: "Don't come here, we will go to you, I promise!" It was then that my father understood the reason why he had immigrated to the country. He knew he had to overcome the difficult situations he was facing to give his daughters and wife a better life. My father worked switching from job to job for several months. He looked only for the ones that paid cash, but unfortunately, they were only temporary.

A little over 2 months after he came to the U.S., Dad found a longtime friend from Chiapas as he was walking back to his place. Dad had told him the struggle he was going through and surprisingly, his friend was able to help with his problem for a while.

"I am so glad I found you, and you told me about your situation," he told Dad.

"You know, I am going back to Mexico for a few months. I want to go spend some time with my parents, and I totally understand the struggle you are going through because I was in your shoes once. I will let you borrow my paperwork so you can work legally while I am out of the country!".

The following day after his friend left, my dad went out with so much faith, and for the first time, he felt secure. He went straight to the closest Staffing near his place and turned in the paperwork at the front desk very happy and excited. Even though he was still the same person, he had to remember a big and important change he had since the moment he got his friend's paperwork: his name was no longer Manuel, but he was now Rodrigo.

As he was sitting in the waiting room for his interview, he started a conversation with the man sitting next to him. He saw many people enter and leave the office; not all of them seemed happy. Suddenly, his chance was presented.

"Rodrigo!" the young lady at the front desk called.

"Rodrigo!" she called for the second time. She got no answer from anyone. Everyone looked around searching for Rodrigo, including my dad. It took him about 3 minutes to realize he was Rodrigo.

They got him a job right away. He started working the following day at a company that made all kinds of paper for school. There, he met an American guy named Bob. My father and Bob became very good friends after his first week; they worked side by side the entire time. Bob spoke perfect Spanish, and according to Dad, he was a great man. They would take turns buying or cooking lunch every day. They were both hard workers and helped each other at their labor. If one of them missed a day, the other would make sure he helped as much as he could, so they didn't get behind.

Bob listened to Dad attentively as he spoke about us and how much we missed each other. After his first two months of working at the company, Dad started to ponder what he would do the following month when his friend Rodrigo came back to the states. He didn't want to tell his problem to anyone, especially Bob. He was afraid Bob would see the situation differently than it was.

As time passed, my mother, sister and I in Mexico started to adapt to the idea that we could not be with Dad anymore, but we had faith that the Lord would reunite us again someday.

Life was tough without Dad for all of us. We missed him in our own ways. Mom was always finding a way to help financially. She would sell food, clean houses, babysit or just cut out some expenses. We had some pretty good neighbors, especially the single mom at the corner of the street. She and Mom became good friends as did her kids and us.

Crimes in Juarez were starting to get out of the normal numbers. Dozens of people were killed each month, and the majority were women. Everyone was afraid to even go out the door. Cartels and gangs were in control of the city.

One night, as Mom stood at the door of our house talking to one of the neighbors, we experienced one of the many crimes that were happening. A young man of about 23 years old ran inside my house to escape from other people that were chasing him. Everything happened so quickly that Mom didn't even see the young man coming. She turned her back for one minute, and that was all he needed to get in the house.

THE STORY OF A DREAMER

Her reaction was fast. After realizing that my sister and I were inside; she grabbed the young man from the back of his shirt and pulled him towards her without even caring if he had a weapon. We stood there frozen watching him pass us as he ran towards the back door of the house. He ran throwing everything that was in his way. Mom and the neighbor chased him to the back patio holding our hands. She stopped as she saw the back door open and her birthday cake upside down on the floor. The young man stopped at our patio door and looked around desperately trying to find a way out. The kitchen was so dark that he hadn't even noticed we were behind him.

Panicking, Mom opened the drawer in the kitchen and pulled out a long knife. As she stood there deciding what to do, three more men entered my house with guns and knives chasing the young man. There were at least 4 innocent hearts that stopped as we saw them coming in carrying weapons. They were all dressed in fancy suits, but that didn't make them less scary. Two of them ran out to the patio following the young man who was doing his best to climb the unfinished stairs to the neighbor's balcony.

We watched with pounding hearts as we saw the neighbor step out of his bedroom to receive the young man with a baseball bat in hands. The young man couldn't get past the neighbor. They trapped him, laid him on his back and then dropped him from the second floor hitting the pavement on the patio. He was very lucky to have been able to get up from there without a scratch; at least that's how he acted. The two men quickly ran down the stairs to assure him. They came back in our house carrying the young man, as the third man in a suit stood there apologizing to Mom about what had just happened.

"He stole something from us, and we had to get him," he explained. "But tell me what he broke, I will pay you for all the damages he caused on your property," he told Mom as he stared at her birthday cake on the floor with his wallet in hands.

"He didn't break anything, just leave and don't come back!" Mom answered him with a voice of mixed feelings. "You just scared the crap out of us, and thanks to you, my daughters are crying!" she told him raising her voice.

He looked at us and walked away slowly. Mom walked behind him making sure they all left the house, she shut the door after the last man and then opened the blinds to see from the window as the black Tahoe drove off with all of them aboard.

Chapter

XIII

*U*nlike us, life in the U.S. for Dad was getting much brighter. His friend Rodrigo didn't show up until five months after he went to Mexico and so he and Bob helped Dad continue to work at the same place. With this benefit, Dad was able to get his own place even though he had no furniture.

A little over a year after Dad migrated to the United States, he and Mom began to plan how to get us to the United States. Neighbors around us were getting killed for no good reason. We had to move four times that year trying to escape danger. Unfortunately, there were only two ways to survive; you either had to join them, or you could run away like we had been doing with the risk of getting killed someday.

Neither one of those two choices were good options for us. One day, as they were taking lunch, Bob confessed to Dad that he had helped a family get to the U.S. before. What a small world! The family he had helped were my aunt and cousins who had lived across the street from us when we lived in Chiapas.

It was surprising to know they lived in Texas; they had disappeared suddenly leaving everything behind, and no one knew where they had gone. Dad dedicated his free time to search for them; It didn't take him too long to find them. According to my aunt, crossing the border with Bob wasn't an issue at all.

"It was very easy," she said. "The scariest part might have been crossing the river. But no worries! People make it sound much scarier than it really is; plus, we grew up going to the river all the time in Chiapas anyways so it can't be scary!"

Dad was very confused; what my aunt had told him was a completely different version of what he had heard from other people. "There is no way it could have been that easy!" he thought. He tried to make my aunt say something that had been terrifying, but she didn't change her words. He went back to his place that night with a big smile across his face. He was completely sure that if my aunt who was old, weak, skinny, and sick made it across the border without a problem, then we could do it too.

It was the end of the school year when Mom and Dad finally decided it was time. It was way too soon for me. I had just finished fifth grade, and it hurt so much that I didn't even get the chance to say goodbye to my friends and teachers. Mom started getting rid of all the things we had in our house. She gave most of the furniture to one of her cousins who had moved to Juarez a few weeks before. We were only allowed to take two suitcases. Among the things she gave her cousin, she included my drawings I had made for Dad. I had been hoping to give him my drawings once we were reunited. When I argued with Mom about it, she lied to me saying her cousin would send us that suitcase with my drawings once we had made it to the United States. That made everything so worth it. But there was no way I could know what we were about to face.

Chapter

XIV

We took a bus to Reynosa, Tamaulipas the night of August 6, 2004; just 3 days after I turned 11. Innocently, my sister and I agreed to obey Mom on everything if we got to see Dad. We knew we were going to him, but we didn't expect to be as hard. Dad and Bob came to an agreement; Bob would bring us all the way to Dad for two thousand dollars each. Dad was working very hard to be able to save all that money. Besides the job at the paper company, he also worked as the maintenance guy for the apartment complex where he lived. He had all kinds of tasks there: he painted apartments, cleaned them, fixed sinks, toilets, windows, or any issue that the tenants might have.

During his lunch breaks, he picked up aluminum cans from the dumpsters and street, so he could sell them and make a little extra money. He was working the entire time, and that man never got tired. He didn't mind sleeping and eating on the floor; he only wanted his family back.

My uncles in Arizona were in contact with Mom. They knew Dad needed help getting money and they offered to help. As Dad worked on saving six thousand dollars, my uncles made sure that Mom had enough money for a hotel, food, and other expenses we might have.

Meanwhile, on the other side of the border, my sister and I were enjoying the 'trip.' We fought about who would get the window seat every time the bus stopped; we both wanted to see the outside. We were going places that we've never been to before. Even though it wasn't the best view, the fact that we were traveling meant the world to us.

Our first home as we arrived at Reynosa, Tamaulipas was the hotel across the street from the bus station. Staying there was a complete luxury for us. We didn't even know what hotels looked like from the inside. As usual, my sister and I fought over who got the remote control for the TV. We soon were at peace when we found out we wanted to see the same thing. We were both enjoying the time up to that point. We loved these 'vacations' on which all we had to do was watch music videos on the TV all day.

On our second day at the hotel, we went down to the restaurant and had breakfast. I always had a good time down there, it was funny to see the customer's reactions when they looked at the long, variable menu repeatedly to find out all they had available were eggs.

Mary, the owner, cook and only waitress of the restaurant, was a hard-working woman and a very sweet lady. She knew most of her customers very well. Even though the restaurant was small, and the menu lacked variety she always had customers.

As Mom and she started a conversation, Mary told her days later that the customers that were at the restaurant most of the time were coyotes. Mom slowly started giving Mary information about what we were there for. She recommended a few coyotes that she had known for years. Mom was conscious of Dad's struggles, so she changed her mind at the last minute and chose the cheapest coyote that she had met days earlier.

The way he painted the panorama was simple and easy: there is no walking at all, you will be sitting in a car the entire time with AC on and I will get you to Dallas early in the morning the next day. Mom trusted him, believing that "they wouldn't take advantage of their own people."

Early in the morning the next day, Mom, my sister and I walked to the bus station across the street from the hotel to wait for the coyote as he had instructed. We saw people enter and leave the bus station every minute. We sat on the bench impatiently for 6 hours hoping the man who had promised to take us to Dad would show up. He never did; he did not answer the phone or come back with an explanation. He had stolen part of the money that my father had worked so hard for.

We went back to the same hotel after that; this time, Mom started working with Mary at the restaurant. Mom taught Mary how to cook some of the dishes from the south. Together, they were able to make the business grow to the point where she allowed us to stay at her house and have free food every day. Mom took the offer to reduce the hotel expenses and help Dad a little bit that way.

Mary's house was small but comfortable. She was a single mother to two daughters who were our same age. We got along with them very well. They were both very friendly girls and very respectful to their mother. They liked to share their dolls with us; which was not very common to see at that age.

During the time Mom worked with Mary, she got to know many people, especially the coyotes to whom she tried to be friendly. They always complimented her food and made her see the impact she had on the restaurant since she started working. After waiting several days to recover hope and trust, Bob and Dad closed a deal between them which involved bringing my mom, my sister and me to the other side of the border.

Bob started moving and contacting his people as soon as Dad gave him half of the money that he would charge for all three of us. Mom worked with Mary until the day Bob picked us up. It was hard to leave them behind. Mary had been our only friend for the couple of weeks we were in Reynosa. Her daughters cried as they hugged us saying goodbye. We thought we'd never see each other again. Our thoughts came and went as we imagined so many things that might happen. Still, we decided to try again.

Chapter

XV

"**Hi! I'm Bob!**" **he said** stretching his hand to Mom. I've always believed that first impressions matter a lot. He was a nice guy, very respectful and attentive. By looking at him, I was sure we would get to Dad's arms quickly and safely. He was big, had pale skin, and blue eyes, and as Dad had mentioned to Mom before, he spoke perfect Spanish.

He was easy to get along with, and it didn't take us long at all to get comfortable with him. As we rode with him, he explained to Mom that he didn't work alone on this 'business.' "Yo no soy la persona que les cruzara el rio. Yo estare esperando del otro lado del muro con mi carro para llevarlos directo a Dallas" I heard him tell Mom.

I should have expected that, but it took me by surprise at first. I also heard him tell Mom that he was driving to the bus station to pick up someone else at my dad's request. We were meeting Linda, a close family member of my dad's cousin, who had decided to cross the border with us at the last minute.

My father's cousin was paying for Linda's trip. Linda was short, dark skin and short curly hair. She was as nice as she looked, and Mom recognized her instantly. Linda came all the way from Chiapas to make the trip and was determined to make it to the other side no matter what. With her, we all felt more protected. At least it wasn't only us. We were comfortable with her as well. We baptized her as our Auntie, and she did for us exactly what an Auntie would have done.

Early the next day, Bob drove us to our starting point. Mom and Auntie took the opportunity to catch up on each other's lives; as my sister and I sat glued to the window admiring the green view.

The road was quite lonely and dirty. In no time, the highway was done, and we were soon driving on a pathway with no pavement. Surprisingly, it felt flatter and much smoother than the one with the pavement. The one-hour drive felt like a 5-minute drive because we were distracted by the view. Bob soon got us to our destination where we would meet the person who would get us across the border.

There was complete silence among us as we stepped out of the car and walked toward the house. It was more like a farm; there were chickens, dogs, and mosquitoes all over the place. We could hear coyotes howling far away.

Mom and Auntie grabbed our hands and slowly followed Bob who was walking quickly toward the house. The 4 of us were scared about what to expect inside the house. We knew what we were about to do was illegal, but the guilt I felt was much bigger.

Chapter

XVI

"*E*sta es la persona que cruzara la frontera con ustedes" Bob introduced his ally. When I looked at him, I was sure we were not going to make it to the other side alive. He was old, early 60's at least; he was skinny and seemed weak. "Por su seguridad, no puedo revelar su verdadero nombre, asi que lo llamaremos 'Chente'" Bob continued.

I was so afraid. I did not want to cross the border with him. Mom, Sister, Auntie, and I stared at Bob as he got back inside the car and drove off taking our suitcases. I just wish we could fit inside them so our ride to the USA would be fast, easy, and painless. "Vayan adentro, la television esta en la sala" Chente demanded as soon as Bob disappeared from our sight.

Very nervously, the four of us followed his command and went inside his house. We all stared at him as he walked to the room across the hallway, pulled out two huge inner tubes and began inflating them. My nerves increased along with the inner tubes. I was really hoping the tube would explode or have a hole, so we could move this to another day. Apparently, Chente lived by himself in the big one-bedroom house. Except for the restroom, none of the rooms had a door.

All four of us sat in front of the TV having no idea what we were watching. We were in a whole different world. I was sure that we were all asking ourselves the same question: "How the heck are we even going to make it to the other side of the river?" No one said a word. We heard nothing but the sounds of the animals outside. Before Bob left, he had assured Mom we were walking no more than 30 minutes.

Around 11am, the old man finished inflating the inner tubes and began cleaning up the patio for his chickens. We were so nervous that we noticed every single movement he made while we were inside. He was acting as if he had all the time in the world.

My sister's expression made me feel even worse. She seemed so afraid. The nervous look in her eyes was something I had never seen in her before. She was looking around way too much as if she could see something that we couldn't. Mom and Auntie were doing their best to try to hide their fear, but their voices betrayed them as soon as they started a conversation. I couldn't stop looking at the old man. A lot was going through my mind, and no matter how hard I tried, I couldn't think of anything else.

At 2 o'clock in the afternoon, he started loading the inner tubes on the back of his old truck. We observed every movement he made. None of us trusted him no matter what Bob had said. We were only allowed to bring with us an extra shirt and a pair of dry pants that we would use once we got to the other side of the river. No food, no water, no lights and since we would be walking among the trees, Bob had asked us to dress in green or black to blend in.

As he walked back into the house, he noticed all of us staring at him. He opened the front door halfway, stopped and instructed in his loud, strong voice: "get in the truck!" Mom and Auntie looked at each other and paused for a second. I started walking backward without losing sight of Chente; something told me he wasn't a good person. My sister was already hiding behind Mom and refused to move one step forward.

In a moment of comfort, Auntie hugged me and whispered to my ear: "Todo va a estar bien, no tengas miedo. Yo te cuidare!" I nodded my head and proceeded to take her hand and walk outside. It was a little harder for Mom to convince my sister, but they eventually came outside to continue.

We stood at the door of his old truck with our plastic bags in hands. I felt like I was being kidnapped. His big greenish eyes made him look like a wild animal about to attack. No one wanted to ride in the front seat with him, but of course, Mom took that risk.

He started driving towards the Rio Grande. The pathway was lonely. There was nothing but rocks, trees, and grass all over the place. We did not see one single person or car around, which made it even scarier. I don't know if it was my imagination, but I began hearing the river in no time as well as the sounds of animals. Louder and louder every time.

He drove without saying a word and often glancing at us using the rear-view mirror, making unfriendly faces. I asked myself while in that truck many questions that I still haven't answered to this day: Why do we have to do this? If we are all brothers and sisters, and God created us equally, why do we treat each other so differently? Why do we even have borders? Why is it so difficult to have a family together? Why is it so easy for Americans to cross the border and visit my country, but I must suffer so much to get to theirs?

I realized after Auntie explained to me that we had to go through this because of the mistakes of others. It just didn't sound fair to me that we all had to face the consequences because one of us messed up. I've thought very hard about it throughout my life, and I still haven't come up with a good reason to treat each other differently. There are good and bad people all over the world. Bad people cannot be identified by one single race, color, or nationality. However, most people believe the opposite.

Chapter

XVII

*A*s the old man kept driving down the lonely pathway, he came across a Mexican soldier who came out of nowhere. He stopped the truck as he saw us and instantly demanded that we get off the truck. My little heart began racing very fast. I knew this could not be good. We were aware that what we were about to do was illegal, and we could go to jail for it. "A donde van?" he asked very seriously.

Mom, Sister, Auntie, and I kept our lips sealed. "I'm going to cross these people who want to get to the other side" the old man replied. I couldn't believe his answer, he just straight up let it go. My whole body started shaking. I had a feeling the old man had set up a trap for us, and this was it. He was turning us in to the police and keeping the money that Dad had given Bob.

"Con permiso de quien?" the soldier asked angrily. "Come on! Don't be so tough on us... You never saw anything" the old man told him handing him some money. The soldier smiled and accepted it. He counted the bills. I couldn't decide if I should be happy or upset by what I was seeing. Is this how our government works? How was I supposed to trust the people that 'protected' my country after this? On the other hand, I thank God he didn't do what he was supposed to. Otherwise, Mom and Auntie would have been put behind bars.

"Tengan cuidado, migracion esta cerca de aqui, vayanse por el otro lado," the soldier said holding the truck's door open for the old man. Realizing the nasty, flirty look that the soldier was giving my sister, the old man quickly got us inside the truck and wrapped up the conversation with the soldier shaking hands.

He continued driving quietly in the same direction for a couple more miles. We didn't see anyone else after the soldier. However, the old man kept decreasing the speed taking a pathway in between the trees until he stopped completely. "We've arrived!" he said getting out the truck.

I could hear the water loudly and clearly, but I was still unable to see the river due to the number of trees around me. I could have sworn I heard a huge waterfall. The old man grabbed the inflated inner tubes from the back of his truck and began walking forward expecting us to follow him.

We walked for a couple of minutes until we hit the right spot to go down to the river. It was like a slide made of mud, once we made our way down, we would be able to see the river. "Tengan cuidado! Es mas rebaloso de lo que se ve" he warned us as he got ready to go down. He threw the inner tubes first, making sure they landed in a dry place. He then sat down and descended all the way down making it seem fun.

"Next, quickly!" He demanded as soon as he got there. Mom quickly sat down and began sliding carefully holding herself tight from the few rocks on the side. She made it there with her pants and part of her shirt completely covered in mud. "Next one!" the old man announced again without even looking. The three of us still up there looked at each other. Neither one of us really wanted to be the next one. In fact, I wanted to run away.

"Vamos! No tenemos todo el dia!" the old man pressed.

"No se preocupen ninas, voy yo primero" Auntie offered. She sat down and without being ready, she slid accidentally, falling all the way down. Mom and the old man quickly helped her get up. "I'm fine!" she yelled to prevent us from feeling more scared. It was a little too late for that. Sister and I were trembling up there; we did not want to move from our place. We knew she was hurt and that was barely the beginning of all.

"Sigues tu!" my sister told me very scared.

"What if we do it at the same time?" I proposed. She agreed right away.

"Andale, sera divertido!" I cheered even though I was terrified. We both sat down slowly and carefully. She sat behind me accommodating her legs and holding herself tight with her arms around my stomach.

"Ready?" I asked.

"Si" she said pausing on her breaking voice. I started moving down slowly keeping us away from the rocks. The old man waited impatiently. "Lo estan haciendo bien!" Mom yelled. My fingers began to hurt from scratching the ground. I could feel my sister breathing very fast. "We are almost there!" I whispered to her. We got down there safely and soundly after a few seconds of sweating. But our eyes were instantly looking at something even worse than our recent descent in the mud.

Chapter

XVIII

The Rio Grande was the most horrible river I'd ever seen in my short life. It was so wide that we couldn't even see the other bank. The water was the nastiest part of it; I couldn't decide what color it was. It had a mixture of green, brown, and black. There were empty plastic bottles of water on the side, empty chip bags, and abandoned kid's clothes; which made me imagine stories about what might have happened to the owner.

My sister started walking backward slowly as if she were going to climb up the hill we had just slid down. Her tears began to fall as she realized there was no turning back. My heart was beating very fast. I couldn't get my eyes off the water; I had never been so scared in my life.

"I want 2 people on each inner tube" the old man instructed paying no attention to us. I raised my eyes searching for God. It felt as if He weren't there anymore. I prayed silently trying very hard not to let my tears come out.

My chest was full of feelings that I couldn't hold for much longer. "Todo va a estar bien!" Auntie said stroking my hair. I began taking long, deep breaths to calm myself down, but it was useless. My tears began as soon as I heard my sister shout out: "Mama, no quiero morir aqui." Her whole body was shaking. She was freaked out still trying to climb up the descent.

She sat there refusing to go near the water. Her tears didn't stop. I was feeling the same way she was, but instead, I cried quietly in my place willing to continue and letting God make the decision about what would happen to us.

"Please! You will see your dad, we will have a better future" Mom begged her. The old man started pushing again quickly saying in his angry tone of voice: "Apurense! Migracion nos va a agarrar si seguimos perdiendo el tiempo." He was right, but I still couldn't believe how heartless and selfish he was. We were only children; of course, we were scared.

I began taking baby steps towards the water until I finally got there. It was freezing! Crossing the border in the middle of November wasn't a good idea. The cold wind made everything even worse. I felt like the river was my end and trying to cross it would be the last thing I would ever do.

As I stepped forward into the water, my foot went all the way down trespassing the ground and making me fall into the water completely. The old man quickly ran into the water as he saw me struggling to keep my head above the surface. The waves in the river that the wind was creating did not help at all. Neither helped my situation. My sister cried even harder as Mom and Auntie ran to my rescue.

Things couldn't get worse. Now I knew we couldn't even stand on the floor of the river because it was all mud. Mom and Auntie ran back to my sister who couldn't control herself. She was sobbing fearfully with her head down on her knees.

It broke my heart to see how much she feared the river. She couldn't take her eyes off it, as if she were waiting for something to come out of there. "Estaremos bien hija, nada malo va a pasar!" Mom said as she cried with her.

I stared at them swallowing my tears and feelings. We all knew there was no turning back at that point. Getting across the river was our only way out. "Get on the inner tubes" the old man demanded angrily. "Mom, please I want to ride the inner tube with you" my sister begged. Mom turned to me with a look in her eyes that told me her heart was breaking.

She couldn't have both of us with her on the same donut, and she also knew that these could easily be the last moments of our lives.

"Esta bien mama, yo ire con tia. Estaremos bien!" I jumped in before she could say anything. The old man put the donuts around us, and we began floating on the freezing river that Thanksgiving Day of 2004.

I closed my eyes and prayed silently as soon as we started moving on the water. "Por favor, no me dejes morir aqui. Quiero llegar a ser alguien en la vida. Dame la oportunidad!" I begged my Lord in my prayers. Per the old man's instructions, Mom and Auntie held hands to keep both donuts together. It looked so risky; the moment they let their hands go, we would be separated.

I continued crying silently as we moved slowly across the river. My sister couldn't stop sobbing, and Mom couldn't see any of our faces as we were both facing opposite directions. Nobody said a word. I just felt the donuts being pulled and I didn't know how it was happening.

The tabulation of the water at the bottom of the river felt very strong. I fought against the strong waves that threatened to drag me down in no time.

"Solo hagan lo que les digo y nada malo sucedera" the old man reminded us before submerging into the water completely. I tried so hard to distract myself with something else and began playing with the water as we kept moving deeper into the river.

The sun was up and bright, but it didn't keep us warm enough. I felt my aunt move her head from side to side watching out for people or any danger we might confront. My tension was increasing by the minute. Nothing felt good about what we were doing, and the fact that I didn't see the old man come out of the water was not a good sign either.

I tried to stay calm and patient. I began to row using my legs as I was still hanging from the donut. The cold wind filled my body with goosebumps. It took the old man a while to get back onto the surface and get some air. I couldn't understand how he was doing it; he had no protection on his body or his face to help him breathe. I couldn't tell how far it was to get to the other side, but I did hear the sound of cars after about 8 minutes on the water.

My sister kept making the river even deeper with her nonstop tears. I was almost sure we would make it to the other side of the river safe and sound after moving in the water for several minutes. Suddenly, I heard helicopters. I wasn't sure the old man could hear it underwater. All four of us began to freak out. We looked up trying to identify the exact location of the helicopter. The next time the old man came out of the water to breathe again, he heard a helicopter and began moving the inner tubes even faster. It took us about 20 minutes to hit the other side of the river.

Luckily, we heard the helicopter fly off, and we were able to come out of the water right away. "Gracias, Dios!" I heard the old man say as he raised his hands to the sky stepping on the dry ground. He quickly bent over and helped my sister get out of the water.

"Welcome to the United States!" he told her as soon as she put one foot on dry ground. My sister's tears stopped slowly once she felt safe.

Mom hugged her as she stepped out of the river. Auntie and I waited impatiently in the water trembling.

Those were some of the worse 20 minutes I had lived in my short life, and our ordeal was not over yet. I wished somebody was waiting for us with a hot cup of tea in their hands. Yeah, that didn't happen. He didn't even bring water. We began changing our clothes as I hid behind the closest tree and changed my pants and shirt. Per the old man's instructions, our wet clothes were left at the side of the river where we changed.

Chapter

XIX

I **could hear border patrol's cars** going from one way to another closer and closer. We started walking as soon as we put our dry clothes on. The day was getting cloudy, and I was beginning to feel colder than before. We were all wearing very thin sweaters; that was all were allowed to bring.

"De aqui en adelante, tienen que tener mucho cuidado" the old man warned before going too far. "We will be walking in between the trees, try not to make any noise when walking, keep up with me at all times in a straight line, and it is very important that the last person erases any footprints we leave" he explained cutting off a set of branches with lots of leaves. "Follow me and do not stop at any time unless I tell you to do so!"

We kept moving in a single line. My sister was behind the old man, followed by my Auntie, me, and my mom who was erasing the footprints. The place was full of trees and green grass that was taller than ourselves. We followed the old man who began walking very fast. Mom was doing her best to keep up and at the same time erasing all the prints. Our ending point was unknown. We saw nothing but more and more trees as we moved forward.

I had no idea how the old man knew we were on the right path. I wondered if he even knew where we were going. It seemed very easy to get lost. He began cutting the pointy branches when we had walked for about 30 minutes; the 30 minutes Bob had promised we were only going to walk. Mom was starting to sneeze constantly. I noticed her red nose when I looked back.

The cold wind, the gray sky, and the wet undies were getting her sick. She was slowing down. The branches were heavy for her. I offered to carry them, but she refused. Noticing we were slowing down, the old man turned around and rushed us. He walked back to Mom, looked at the ground, and said angrily: "You are not erasing the prints completely! Pay attention to what you are doing!" It hurt me to hear the way he was talking to Mom. But there was absolutely nothing I could do; he was in charge, and no matter how hard it was to admit it, he could do many things against us if we created a conflict with him.

I swallowed my words and kept moving. I just wished I was strong enough to carry Mom, so she didn't have to walk. Auntie gave him an unhappy look as he walked past her, then took the branches from Mom and kept moving forward erasing the prints. We continued following the old man hearing border patrol's cars closer each time.

"We are almost there!" he whispered after several more minutes of walking. How did he even know? I could see nothing different. It was impossible to tell what our ending point was when all we could see were grass and trees. I was really beginning to think he was lost. The pathway where he was taking us had no sign of people stepping there before, and if he claimed to have taken people across the border before, wouldn't he use the same pathway?

I felt goosebumps all over my body. My clothes were not a bit dry, and the cold wind was making me thirsty. About 45 minutes had gone by since we had crossed the river. We soon came across a crossing pathway that migration drove on with their cars. The old man stopped right before he stepped on the sandy pathway, looked on both sides and continued walking at the same speed.

We took about 3-4 steps when out of nowhere, one of the border patrol's cars came out of the trees. That was all they were waiting for; just a small noise so they could catch people.

"Corran!" the old man yelled as he began running in between the grass.

He ran very fast trying to get himself safe from getting caught. My sister ran right behind doing her best not to lose him. I turned back and realized Mom was having a hard time. Auntie ran behind pushing her forward. I knew Mom was trying very hard but at the speed she was running I was sure we'd be caught easily. At least, she wasn't giving up yet.

I stopped and retraced my steps to help Mom. Noticing that, my sister stopped and helped her as well. That made us lose the old man who didn't even bothered to look back. "No lo pierdan!" Mom pointed out to us. My sister and I ran behind him trying to get a sign of which way he might have gone until we finally saw him again. "There he is!" my sister whispered as we kept running on the grassy pathway.

We kept our eyes on him and blocked everything else. Unfortunately, my sister was running so fast that didn't realize a big hole coming up and fell straight inside it. Since I was following her at the same pace, I fell after her and hurt her right leg. Mom and Auntie made the same mistake and hurt her leg even more as they fell on top of us.

She let out a quick scream and then covered her mouth with both hands. Her leg was not broken, but she was in a lot of pain and wasn't able to get up right away. "vamos, levantate!" my mom begged as she helped her stand up. She tried, but she was able to only take a few steps before she fell to the ground again. "Necesito descansar un poco!" she asked Mom. We quickly helped her stand up and hid behind one of the biggest and closest trees we saw. Mom helped her stretch her leg as we sat down to catch our breath. Ants quickly ran to our bodies from the trees and underground.

Auntie sat there nervously looking around expecting to find something more dangerous than just ants. We sat there trying to decide what in the world we would do in the middle of the forest without the old man.

The environment became so quiet that I could hear my own heartbeat. "Vamos a esperar unos minutos mas hasta que nos aseguremos de que migracion ya no esta por aqui" Mom suggested in a whisper. I wish I could have the same faith she did at that moment. Although I didn't say anything, I knew immigration was not going away. They knew someone was around and their goal was to catch those people.

We waited for about 20 minutes under that tree. Our bodies were getting colder. The ants were killing us, but at least their bites helped keep us warm. We heard border patrol's cars moving away as if they were leaving. Mom stood up very slowly and took a few steps north, east, south, and west double checking that there was nobody around. When she came back convinced that they were gone, we all stood up and began walking by ourselves.

Chapter

XX

We walked blindly, having no idea where the pathway we were taking would lead us. My sister was limping, but she was not giving up. We all kept her pace taking her into consideration. The tall grass kept going on and on. We could still hear cars in the distance, and as we kept moving, we began to hear voices. We followed the voices and noise we heard having faith that they would get us somewhere.

About 15 minutes after we began exploring alone, we heard noises in the grass that we were not making. We froze for a second making no noise at all as we tried to guess what was coming toward us. Whatever it was, it was moving very fast and coming directly to us. My sister turned her neck around facing the closest tree and said full of fear: "una culebra!".

We all turned to the tree she was pointing to and noticed a nasty snake swinging at the end of a branch. We instantly realized what could be coming towards us at that speed and began running after my sister who was terrified. We didn't say a word or even try to stop her. I would have preferred that immigration find us to getting bitten by that horrible reptile.

We walked desperately searching for a way out of the grass, and we decided to turn ourselves in. My sister's tears didn't stop as she kept running in a straight line towards nowhere. "Follow the voices, honey. We must find immigration. They will help us" Mom told her without even trying to keep her voice down this time.

We all had agreed to find immigration or let them find us, but God had a different plan. Before we could find our way out of the grass, we came across the old man as we ran, driving him straight to the ground. He had come back to look for us. The moment we saw him we were not a bit happy. We were over this trip already and over his rude attitude. But there was something different in him this time that motivated us not to give up yet.

He was acting kind and even helped my sister to walk as he noticed she was hurt. Even his tone of voice had changed.

Mom decided to give him another opportunity since he was helping us get to Dad. It took us about 20 more minutes before we could step on clear ground again where there was no grass, and we could see our pathway.

As we emerged from the grass, we came across a small hill that was just meters away from where we were standing. As the old man had instructed, we threw ourselves to the ground and started moving with our stomachs down. We followed him all the way to the top of the hill holding the same position. We could hear voices and the sound of cars near us, but we couldn't see what was behind the hill yet.

As we made it to the top, the old man instructed not to lift our heads. "Vamos directo a ellos!" he warned in a whisper. He was right. We began lifting our heads up slowly to notice that behind the hill, about a mile away there was a whole congregation of Border Patrols, having what appeared to be a lunch break.

We could hear laughs and even music coming from the small building where they had gathered. The building was surrounded by brick walls in the back, and on the left, and right, but it was completely open from the side from which we observed them.

"This is our final point" the old man explained. "Bob va a estar detras de ese edificio en cualquier momento."

We waited there in the same position expecting to see Bob drive behind the building anytime. Noticing it was getting late and that Bob hadn't shown up, the old man reached in his pocket and pulled out a flip phone. "Donde estas, Bob?" he whispered as he dialed Bob's phone number. We heard the phone ring a few times getting no answer at the other end of the line.

Our stomachs began growling from hunger; my mouth was so dry, and I'm sure everyone else's was too. As we laid there without moving, I began to feel sleepy. My body was getting colder, and my energy was running out. I slowly put my head down on the ground giving a sign that I was about to give up. I needed at least water to keep going. The old man kept trying to contact Bob when suddenly, we heard a helicopter coming our direction. "Bajen las cabezas y no se muevan!" the old man warned.

We did as he told us, but believe it or not, it was hard to stay still. My whole body began to shake. The helicopter flew near us and then away. My sister begged for a drop of water as she began closing her eyes. I felt how one by one we began to pass out slowly.

"Se quedarian aqui a salvo mientras voy a traer agua?" Chente asked. We all looked at him saying nothing with our heads on the ground. "He must be kidding!" I thought. We were right in front of the border patrol crew, how did he expect us to stay there 'safely'? But we were too weak to argue.

"If you stay here quietly without moving, nothing bad will happen" he suggested.

"Agua!" my sister whispered with her eyes halfway open. She was the weakest of all. Her body didn't move, and her face was turning pale. I didn't think the old man was coming back after this. How was he going to bring us water? Or even worse, where was he going to get it from?

"Adelante!" Mom told him not very convinced. "Regresare, lo prometo!" he said getting up slowly.

Mom rubbed her hands on my sister's back trying to give her some heat while Auntie did the same thing with me. We all laid there willing to take a nap and didn't even bother to spy on immigration anymore. The last thing I remember before closing my eyes completely was Mom falling asleep.

I tried so hard to stay awake, but I couldn't. I don't know how long we were asleep, but I do remember being the last one to wake up. As I opened my eyes slowly, I noticed Mom having a worried expression on her face. She was trying hard to listen to the voices she was hearing. She put her finger across her lips a couple of times indicating she wanted complete silence from us.

I started to hear the same thing she was after a few seconds. I could hear two people talking in the distance. The voices were getting closer every time. As we lifted our heads up, we spotted two young men coming up the hill in our direction. They had no idea we were right there, and they seemed to have walked from the immigration building.

One of them had a backpack with him. "Bajen la cabeza! No se muevan! No hagan ruido!" Mom whispered very nervously. I began praying with my head on the ground. That was about the only thing I could do at that moment. We all had given up already, we knew there was no way out of this one. It was a little too late to move and hide, so we didn't even attempt that. We were just waiting for them to come to us and resisting until the last second. I began sweating. I was very afraid. There was complete silence from everyone as I felt them standing right in front of me.

Chapter

XXI

"**W**hat are you doing here!?**" one of them asked loudly. I lifted my head slowly to look at him, while Mom did the same thing. We said nothing. We were not mentally ready to answer his questions.

"Who brought you here?" the other one jumped in.

"We got here by ourselves!" Mom answered sounding frightened.

They both laughed at Mom's answer and said: "Yeah, right! Do I look that stupid to you?" in a louder tone of voice.

I felt I was running out of oxygen. I was very scared just thinking about all the trouble we would be in after this.

"You don't have to believe me!" Mom said bothered by their laughs. The two young men stood there laughing even harder at Mom's answers to their questions; they appeared to be enjoying making her angry.

"No se enoje, Doña!" they finally said more respectfully. "I know it was that stupid old man" he continued.

"I don't know who you are talking about!" Mom said looking away from them.

"I know because he is my uncle!" he said seriously. "But don't worry! I am not a border patrol or I won't call them on you either. Just be careful because they are everywhere!" he warned us walking away. We never knew who they were, or if what they said was true, but I did conclude that his rudeness level was about the same as the old man's, which made sense to me that they were related.

We began to lose patience after that. We looked around from our spot trying to spot the old man and immigration. Most of the border patrol agents hadn't moved from the building, but the few that did were already spreading and going back to their spots. Our nerves increased every minute with their movements. My dry mouth was getting even dryer, and the grassless ground didn't protect us a bit from the cold. I don't know what everyone else's plans were, but I wasn't planning on spending the night in that place.

It took the old man about an hour to get back, according to him. It felt more like 5 hours to us, but we were incredibly grateful that he had come back as he had promised. He brought with him a 500mL bottle of water to share. Don't know where he got it from and honestly, I was so thirsty that I wasn't even concerned about that. Mom quickly handed the bottle to my sister. The 3 of us stared at her as she began taking a couple of drinks. I was very afraid she would end up finishing it. She stopped right when she noticed our mouths open, wishing for a zip of it. Mom and Auntie took good care of the water. They didn't drink much to make sure there was some more for later since we didn't know how much longer we had to wait.

The bottle was more than half empty by the time we all had a chance to take a drink. "I was also able to communicate with Bob" the old man whispered. He should be here any minute. The clock moved along with the sun as it was coming down. Bob was not showing up, and we were starting to get worried. Immigration started driving their cars away from the building ready to catch some people, but not all of them left. There were about 8 border patrol agents left in the building, who were not planning on moving.

"Tenemos que salir de aqui" the old man said concerned about forty-five minutes later. We followed him as he crawled down the hill again and began walking east climbing on some big rocks. The rocks looked very harmful as if they were there on purpose. We made it past the rocks without a problem, but we didn't get too far when we heard the helicopters once again. The old man started running as he heard the helicopter wander around closely. "No paren hasta llegar al monte!" he instructed.

We ran with him as fast as we could. There were no trees or grass where we could hide. Everything was clear ground and easy to see from the air. With a lot of effort and running out of breath, we came across a huge hole on the ground. We began making our way down the hole when the old man quickly threw himself into the tall grass that was on the right side of the hole. Auntie and Mom followed him and covered themselves with the grass. My sister and I hid behind a big rock that blocked the view from the front of the hole, and it also blocked the view from above as there was a tree right in front of us.

We all stayed there quietly for a couple of minutes as we heard the helicopter wander around us. My sister and I closed our eyes tightly and put our heads down. We were trying so hard that it was impossible for us to stay still. I felt my sister's body shake constantly.

When the old man felt it was safe, he came out of the grass and so did Mom and Auntie. I looked around carefully. A few meters away from me, there was a small puddle of water. Right in front of that, there were a couple of dried trees and little rocks everywhere. There was really no place to hide in that hole other than the spots we had already taken.

The old man crawled back to the top of the hole making sure immigration was really gone. From up there, he could see the exact spot where Bob would be waiting with the car. There was still no sign of him.

"Algo no esta bien!" the old man whispered back down. "You will have to excuse me for a couple more minutes. My phone is not picking up signal and I need to talk to Bob" he said. "Stay here and make sure you are out of sight!" he told us before leaving once again.

Mom got up and cleared our spot of any rocks that might seem uncomfortable where we were sitting. I wish she could have stayed with us, but the rock was only big enough to cover two people. She kissed our cheeks and then walked bravely back to the grass with Auntie to lie down again. My mind couldn't stop thinking about how much risk they were running on that grass. That's where snakes like to hide.

I wanted to cry so bad, I just wanted to go home; away from trouble. My sister had an "I give up" face on her. She turned her body away from me and closed her eyes. My whole body trembled; that place was even colder than where we were before. My tears started coming down one after another. I was very careful not to make any noise. That place was so quiet that you could hear a pin drop. I rubbed myself to make some heat; at least my tears were hot enough to warm up my face.

Everyone but me fell asleep in no time. Instead, I played with the insects that crawled on my body. Our stomachs began growling as they all slept. I giggled at the noises; that was about all I could do. Sitting there immobile was making me lose hope. I tried to remind myself of the reason we were doing this and started feeling tired as my thoughts began to flow. My eyes felt heavy. I was trying so hard not to close them. I wanted to watch out for animals and immigration as Mom, my sister, and Auntie slept, but I couldn't keep my eyes open for too long.

I fell asleep deeply finding a comfortable position leaned against the rock. I don't remember what was on my mind before waking up, but I do remember that a horrible snake jumped at me and opened its poisonous mouth, which was the reason I woke up. The time I was asleep could have been no more than twenty minutes, and I was already having nightmares. Along with that image of the snake, I was also watching a fast-forward video of everything I had lived during the last couple hours.

I woke up terrified with my heart pounding and with a start. Everyone else slept still. I could hear Mom and Auntie snoring. I quickly looked around searching for snakes. I turned to my sister who seemed to be knocked out. Making sure she was okay, I hit her softly with my elbow. She answered instantly with a punch on my arm and a frowny face without opening her eyes. I grabbed a couple of insects and began playing with them once again. With the rocks near me, I began making them 'a house'; I thought it would help protect them from the cold a little.

When I was about halfway done with the house, I heard voices again. My heart started beating quickly. Mom and Auntie were still snoring, and it was getting louder. I whispered trying to get Mom's attention, but it was useless. I was afraid to get up. I didn't know exactly where the voices were coming from or how close they were.

The only one I could wake up was my sister, who was sleeping right next to me. I quickly woke her up without making any noise. As soon as she opened her eyes, I warned her not to say a word and to listen. She got very nervous and afraid as she heard the same thing I was hearing. "Nos van a encontrar si mama y tia no dejan de roncar" I whispered to her.

She took a glance at the grass where Mom and Auntie were.

"Throw this to Mom!" she said giving me a rock.

"Estas loca?" I whispered back. "She will kill me! I can crack her head open with this!"

"Tratalo!" she advised very worriedly. I began throwing rocks at Mom as my sister handed them to me. I could not see her, but I was calculating the spot where I thought her leg would be.

After several rocks, Mom finally stopped snoring. We all kept silent for several minutes as we suddenly stopped hearing the voices. My body trembled as I heard steps coming from the top of the hole. I covered my mouth with both hands as I felt somebody stand at the top of the hole looking down. The small rocks fell down the slope. My sister and I didn't move. We were afraid even to breathe. Our eyes didn't move either; we sat there looking straight ahead and hoping we wouldn't get caught.

"Did you find something?" I heard a voice ask. The silence on his end was increasing our fear even more. I was praying our stomachs wouldn't betray us at that moment. His silence in response to the question felt eternal. I heard as they threw an empty bottle of water which landed near me. It really scared me, but I didn't make any noise. My sister began tearing up, and I signaled her to be quiet. She was very scared, and I bet so were Mom and Auntie.

"No, there's nothing here" he finally responded walking away.

Chapter

XXII

bout an hour had passed by since the old man left us in the hole. I was getting very uncomfortable. My butt was hurting from sitting on that same spot for too long. The old man was taking so long, and we had to wait for him no matter what. He was our only way out.

My stomach was hurting, I was so hungry. This wasn't exactly how an 11-year old wished to spend her Thanksgiving Day. It had been the worse day of my life.

I played with the small rocks to kill time making shapes in the ground. Hearts were the main shape I drew. I was halfway done with my fifth heart when I heard a helicopter coming our way once again. "No se muevan!" Mom warned from the grass. I put the small rocks on the ground and leaned my whole body against the big rock not really doing much this time to avoid being visible from the helicopter.

The helicopter wandered above us for a few minutes and then flew away. I heard my sister begin crying once again quietly. I didn't have any more words to console her. I ignored her suffering and didn't even bother to turn her way to look at her.

I had a feeling the helicopter had seen me, and honestly I was really hoping they would come quickly to find us. I was feeling hopeless. I didn't want to continue. Then, just when I thought things couldn't get any worse, I heard steps coming down the slope. I didn't know right at that moment if I really meant my previous thoughts. I wrapped my hands around my knees putting my head down and began crying silently. My sister did the same thing. All my emotions came together as I heard the steps get closer to us each time.

I began shaking once again. A strong headache soon arose. I felt as someone stood by my side staring at me. I cried even harder this time letting my feelings out when I felt a person put his hand on my head and said in a soft tone of voice: "Ya no llores! Vine a sacarte de aqui!" I didn't even have the guts to face him. I was very scared, and I felt like the biggest loser.

"Levantate y vamos a terminar!" he added. I lifted my head up slowly and noticed the old man wiping his eyes. I knew from the bottom of my heart that those words hadn't come exactly from him. I was very sure there had been divine intervention, and it wasn't exactly the old man who had spoken to me. His words gave me the strength and courage to get up and continue, as he had commanded.

The old man helped me get up and then did the same with my sister. "I'm sorry I took too long, but everything is ready now" he apologized.

We climbed out of the hole following him once again. We looked around for any danger as we laid on our stomachs and then he explained: "You see that gray car back there?" he said pointing to a car a bit far from where we were; right behind the immigration building. "That's Bob!" he said. "Now, the only way to get there is to run without stopping and crossing the barbed wires before border patrol sees you."

We looked at him as if he had lost his mind. How were we supposed to get there without catching migration's eyes when we were running toward them? Plus, the land from the hole forward was clear. There was no grass, trees or even rocks where we could hide. "I'm sorry but my job is done at this point. I can't help any further. I'll be watching you all from here" he said.

"Whenever you are ready!" he called. The four of us stood on our feet slowly and stretched a little getting ready to finish this nightmare. I looked at the old man and thanked him for coming back.

"Good luck!" he responded with a slight smile.

We began running when we all were ready. I kept my eyes trained in front of me and on the building not even paying attention to what I was stepping on. I was getting even more thirsty as I ran with my mouth open. Mom was the very last one running behind all of us. My sister ran in the front as fast as she could still limping, trying to stay out of sight from the building.

Bob began moving as we got closer to the wire. My legs were getting so weak after barely a couple minutes of running. Then, I fell into one of the immigration's traps. I stepped on a glass bottle covered on mud and slipped falling backward with my whole back hitting the ground. I was very hurt, and it took a few seconds for my head to go back to normal again. Auntie who was right behind me helped me get up, and I continued running as I could.

I turned back to notice the old man running in the opposite direction, always turning back to observe us. When my sister and I finally made it to the wire, we were out of breath. Bob was only a few meters away now. We tried crossing the barbed wires alone, but they were so close to each other that we needed someone to hold it for us. As we waited impatiently for Mom and Auntie to get there, I lifted the wires up to let my sister cross to the other side. I was so weak that I could barely hold up the wire for her, but it was enough to let her get across.

She waited right there for the rest of us and then Bob redirected her to get in the car. She obeyed and ran to the car leaving the door open. In the distance, I noticed that Bob was not driving alone. There was somebody else with him. But I was more worried about getting there. We were now right next to immigration's building. Only a wall separated us, and so far, it seemed like we were winning.

I crossed the pointy, sharp wires nervously already bleeding from one of them going in my arm. On my attempt to begin running to the car, I fell and instantly heard the alarms on the other side of the building go off. Auntie quickly crossed the wires as Mom held them for her and from the other side, she held the wires for Mom to cross. She had one leg on the other side of the wire when one of the border patrols came out of the building and yelled, "Illegals!"

"Corre!" I read Mom's lips as she told Auntie.

My desperation as I was waiting in the car grew immensely within a few seconds. Mom was stuck on the wires. Her sweater and hair were glued to the barbed wires, and the border patrol was coming after her. Without thinking about it, I tried opening the car's door to go help her, but Bob had locked them to keep me from getting out.

My anger and desperation turned against Bob who was not doing a thing to help Mom and was not letting us help her either.

"Dejame salir!" I yelled at him losing control. I saw from the window as the rest of the agents came out of the building to arrest Mom.

"I'm sorry but I had instructions before the trip began to take you two to Dallas with or without her" Bob explained. My heart was breaking. Bob began moving the car slowly once Auntie got inside.

I watched as the car kept moving when one of the agents got to Mom and grabbed her arm. I saw Mom push him to the ground and pull herself out of the barbed wires ripping her sweater, her pants, and a lot of her hair. "Wait! She's coming!" my sister yelled as she cried hard.

Mom started running to the car as Bob stopped completely and unlocked the doors. The hug I gave her that evening was one of the most special ones. There was no doubt that the Lord had stood with us throughout this trip the entire time. Happily, and angry at the same time, Bob stepped on the gas leaving all the border patrol agents behind.

Chapter

XXIII

As Bob drove us to a hotel, my sister and I looked out the window excited that this country would now be our new home. Best of all, we would be with Dad in a few hours, and this time it would be forever.

I could see why people liked America so much. I had only been there for a few minutes, and I already liked it. This country had taller buildings everywhere, wider roads, lots of flowers everywhere and it hurt to say, but it was much, much cleaner than Mexico.

In the car, Bob's sister rode in the front seat. She was very serious and didn't tell us her name. She didn't talk much, and when she did, she only spoke to Bob in English. We had no clue what she was saying, but I remember it was my first time hearing another language and I was fascinated by it.

By the time we made it to the hotel, it was completely dark. About 9:30pm to be exact. We took turns showering as Bob handed us some dry clothes to wear. Our underclothes never got dry, and we still had to use the same ones since that was the only thing that Bob didn't have for us. Bob and his sister left us alone at the hotel while they went out to bring us some food.

They came back with the biggest tray of food I had seen in my life and sat it on the desk. It all looked delicious! As we ate, Bob told us about Dad. He was just as excited as we were that in just a few hours, we would be reunited with him.

My smile grew as I imagined that special moment. I couldn't wait to hug my father again. My heart was filled with happiness every time I reminded myself of our next stop. As we got ready to leave the hotel, I began putting my shoes back on when Bob looked at me and asked: "Why are your shoes so dirty and ripped?" I felt embarrassed by his question and just smiled saying nothing. Mom explained to him that those were the only shoes we had and since we had been walking all day, they had become even uglier.

He looked at us and instantly said: "Put them in the trash, I'll get each of you a new pair before we make it to Dallas."

His sister did not like the idea. She began arguing with him as soon as he finished his sentence; in English, of course! We did not have to understand exactly what she was saying to know she was against Bob's proposition.

Mom interrupted their argument and said: "No worries, Bob! We can still wear these. When we get to Dallas, I'm sure my husband will get us another pair."

"Of course not!" he insisted. "I can't bring you to Manuel looking like this!" he said. He grabbed all our shoes and tossed them in the trashcan inside the hotel room.

It was about an 8-hour drive to Dallas. Dad knew we were on our way, but he didn't know exactly where we were. I bet he was home feeling very anxious and not sleeping. Bob did his best to fit everyone into the 4-door car he was driving. Since I was the little one, they sat me up front between him and his sister. While he drove, her attitude toward us changed. "Estas anciosa por ver a tu papa?" she finally asked me.

She had very beautiful eyes. Her long, red hair made her look very mean, but there was an angelical side to her. Bob had music on the entire time. He said it helped him to avoid falling asleep. After 40 minutes on the road, Bob told us about what was coming up. "We are about to go through a checkpoint here in a couple more miles. But no worries, all you have to do is say: 'American Citizen'" he explained.

We all went mute for a minute. "What does that even mean?" I thought. A feeling of nervousness soon began growing in my stomach. "Vamos a practicar" Bob's sister told me. I tried repeating after her, but it sounded so different, and there was no way I would get perfect at it in just a few minutes under pressure.

I could already see the checkpoint office as the car kept moving forward. My nerves arose very fast once again. "Is there another option?" Mom asked Bob as we got in line to be checked. "Yes, Just pretend you are sleeping!" he said hesitating.

I liked that idea much better than the previous one. "Close your eyes and do not open them" were Bob's last words before getting to the agent. I closed my eyes quickly pretending to be asleep. They kept moving left to right for some reason even as they were closed. I listened to every single thing they were saying, but I did not understand a word. I felt as a strong flashlight was pointed directly at my eyes. I couldn't help making a gesture showing it bothered me, but I still did not open my eyes.

The woman at the checkpoint turned the flashlight to the back seat looking at Mom, Auntie, and Sister who pretended to be sleeping as well. She asked Bob several questions that I could tell were questions by her tone of voice and Bob's hesitation in responding. She held the flashlight on us for a while. It made me nervous. It was getting harder to pretend I was sleeping. She went back to the conversation with Bob and then he began shaking me trying to 'wake me up.'

"Hey, hey!" I heard him say as he shook my left arm. The movements he did were getting very abrupt to the point that he was hurting me. It was obvious that the immigration agent had noticed that I was faking sleep. I started moving a little without opening my eyes giving it a second try. There was a storm going on in my head at that moment, including Bob's last words to me: "Do not wake up!"

It was a real struggle trying to keep my eyes shut. The way he shook my arms made me think they had already caught our lie. "Hey!" Bob's sister called as she began shaking me as well. The agent didn't move the flashlight from my face. I was beginning to sweat. I opened one eye just barely as I heard the agent walk away. To my surprise, three more agents were walking toward the car with her.

Everything happened so quickly that we didn't have a chance to talk to each other while we waited inside the car. All four of them talked to Bob, one at a time, and then I felt as the car started moving again. My heart was jumping in excitement to think that God had saved us one more time and we were set to continue to Dad's arms.

But it wasn't that easy. As the car began moving, I opened one eye completely and noticed Bob driving towards the parking lot. Next thing I know, two of the agents opened both doors to the back seat "waking up" my sister. They asked her something in English and without having a clue of what they had said, her reply was: "American Citizen." They both laughed hard at the same time.

"Salgan del carro" the agent instructed.

Very scared, we all got out of the car one at a time and with our heads down; we formed a straight line in front of them. Noticing that we had no shoes on, the agents pointed to our feet and laughed even harder. We kept our heads down and said nothing. I felt like I didn't even have the right to look at them, after all; it was their land.

I turned to see the female agent who had stopped us at the beginning. She was the only who was not laughing. Instead, she stared at my sister and me with a look of sorrow. I know she was feeling very sorry for us and deep inside, I knew she didn't want all this to happen. She seemed bothered and annoyed with her coworkers' reactions.

Meanwhile, two other officers investigated Bob and his sister as they handcuffed them. They prevented him or his sister from looking at us after that. The floor was cold, and I did what I could to keep my feet off the ground. "Siganme!" one of the agents finally commanded as he began walking to the entrance of the building. The other two officers followed behind us still laughing.

As we headed to the entrance, I could see lots of people from many countries inside. Not everyone looked Hispanic. The one that really caught my attention was a young, Asian girl sitting in a corner crying silently. She was alone. I looked at her feet and noticed she was barefoot as well, but unlike us, her feet were covered in blood.

My heart was filled with emotions as I started imagining what she could have gone through. She had had a longer and more painful trip than us; that was for sure. My soul ached letting out a deep sigh as I saw her tears falling. I wish I had been old and brave enough back then to have sat next to her and given her a hug and words of comfort that she needed at that moment.

Every immigrant in that building was facing down, having given up, with no sign of hope. On our cold seat, Mom held our hands tightly. We were sitting right in front of the immigration agents. Only a glass window separated us. Mom listened attentively to the questions they asked other people. She wanted to make sure she was ready to respond when it was her turn.

In a moment of silence, we heard one of the agents ask an immigrant: "who is he?" Mom quickly reacted and very discretely, she whispered in my ear: "if they ask you who they are, tell them we don't know them; they picked us off the street and gave us a ride" she instructed referring to Bob and his sister, as she pretended to be fixing my earrings.

The story sounded very fake, but that was the first thing that came to her as a way of saving Bob and his sister from going to jail. It took immigration a while to get to us. When they finally did, one of the agents asked each of us for our names.

"Where are you from?" was his following question as his voice became louder and harsher.

"Mexico!" Mom and Auntie answered at the same time. He stared at Auntie for a second with an unhappy face and then said: "You are not from Mexico!"

"Tell me the truth!" he paused.

Auntie laughed and said: "I am!"

"What part of Mexico?" he grilled.

"Chiapas, Mexico!" she said seriously.

He did not believe her no matter what she said. "Show me your ID!" he demanded.

"I don't have it with me," Auntie told him getting bothered.

He looked at her angrily. He wanted to hear her say that she was not Mexican. "Then you must know... Who is Mario Moreno? Or Xavier Lopez?"

"I don't know" she responded.

All Mexicans, even I knew that those people were very famous Mexican celebrities and that they were better recognized by their nicknames "Cantinflas and Chabelo!"

"Sing the National Anthem then" he pushed her.

"Cough, cough... okay, here we go... One, two, three..." she said moving her arms as if she was directing an orchestra. That was pissing him off. He was getting even more serious, but he stood there quietly as Auntie sang the whole anthem to him.

Even though it was correctly sung, he still did not believe her. "Give me your ID, or I will deport you to Honduras!" he said unpleasantly. Auntie started laughing to his face; and making him even angrier she said sarcastically: "I would forever be grateful to you! I've always wanted to visit Honduras, so this is a good opportunity you are giving me."

The officer looked away appearing to have given up on Auntie and then asked Mom, "Are they your daughters?"

Yes!" She answered firmly.

"How old are they?" he asked.

"Eleven and twelve" she answered.

"You, you and you come with me" he said pointing to Mom, Auntie, and my sister.

I was very scared to be left alone. I was sure they were separating us.

"Where to?" Mom asked nervously.

"Down the hallway!" he instructed. Mom got up slowly while staring at me. She knew I was afraid and the last thing she wanted was to leave any of us alone.

"You will be back in a few minutes" he added.

Before they exited the first door, another officer came to meet my sister. "What about her?" he asked referring to me. "She is too little. Does not meet the required age" he said.

I watched as Mom and Auntie disappeared from the hallway, but they took my sister to a different room. It was a room that was made of glass, right across the hallway from where I was sitting. The officer sat her inside next to some more immigrants who all looked Mexican to me, and then walked away. She was the only child in the room. The people around her started to talk to her while there was no officer inside. They looked down as she talked and nodded their heads.

After several minutes, a different officer went into the room. He was white. He walked straight to my sister and with one hand against the wall, he started asking her questions. He seemed angry. Everyone in the room, including my sister, faced the floor the entire time. They seemed scared.

In my seat, I hugged myself to stay warm. More and more people came into the building. I turned back to see Bob who was sat in the same spot next to his sister. One of the officers interviewed them. I was trying very hard to listen to what he was saying, but my attention was instantly interrupted when I heard an officer scream madly. It was the same officer talking to my sister.

"Tell the truth!" he screamed at her.

I was instantly in panic. I sat tightly in my spot hoping that my sister could hold off on telling him the truth. His anger led him to the point where he began to kick the metal wall to scare her even more.

"If you don't tell me the truth, I will put you in jail for ten years! You won't get out of here until you are 25!" I heard him threaten her.

Every person in the room faced the floor admitting they were terrified as the agent continued kicking and punching the wall. In a moment of silence, my sister; Violeta was brave enough to raise her sight, and looking at him straight in the eyes, she yelled back at him: "I am telling you the truth! I don't care if you don't believe me. I am not afraid of you! And something else, 12 plus 10 is not 25! Re learn your math!"

I was very surprised by her reaction. And all the people inside the room were too. The officer hit the walls even harder and was left speechless. He looked at her very mad and then walked out of the room.

As soon as they saw him disappear, all the immigrants inside celebrated. They clapped and smiled admiring the braveness of a 12-year-old immigrant. I observed as the border patrol agents gathered together in what appeared to be a meeting between them in the hallway. Some of them looked angry; Including the white officer who had interviewed my sister.

As I turned to look at the door, I saw the lady who had stopped Bob's car come in the building. She gave me a quick glance and then walked straight to the meeting. Even there, she couldn't stop looking at me. I felt like they were talking about me. I was getting scared. I turned away to avoid becoming more nervous. There was not one peaceful point at which I could look. Everything around me made me want to cry. It broke my little heart to see people suffer so much.

I slowly put my hands around my knees and then put my head down. It was one of those moments where I thought looking at the darkness was better than keeping my eyes open. As I kept my head down and my eyes closed, I felt someone place a soft palm on my back. I slowly lifted my head up and noticed that same lady.

Her uniform read "Amber." She got on her knees to look in my eyes and then said, "Don't worry! You will be okay. This is for you!" She said holding a small lollipop in her hand. I wanted to be mad at her since she was the one who got us out of the car, but I couldn't. She was too sweet, and her soft voice made me want to hug her instead. She was just doing her job.

I looked straight into her hazel eyes and accepted the lollipop shyly.

"Is that your sister inside?" she asked me as she pointed to her. I nodded without opening my mouth.

"You look alike!" she said smiling. I was wondering what she pretended to do. She was too nice to me, and even though I liked it, I couldn't really trust her.

"Can I ask you a question?" she continued. I didn't say a word or move my head this time. I was afraid of what she was about to ask.

"Who are those people?" she said. Pointing to Bob and his sister.

"I don't know" I whispered.

"You don't know?" You were in the same car with them," she reminded me.

"We don't know them. They found us on the road and gave us a ride" I said.

She thought for a second and then said in the same sweet tone of voice, "They must be very nice people for helping you guys! But... are you sure?" I lifted my head and looked into her eyes and answered, "Yes, very sure. They are good people. Neither one of them is a criminal. Let them go please!" I begged.

Amber wiped the first tear coming out of my eyes and with her eyes still on me, she promised me she would. She walked over to the person who seemed to be her boss and talked to him for a few minutes. She pointed at me, and then to Bob and his sister outside. They walked outside together, and from inside the building I saw as they untied them. They quickly took back the stuff immigration had taken out of the car and giving me a last look, they continued their path forward without us. We let them go expecting to see them again, but they had a completely different plan.

Chapter

XXIV

y the time Mom, Auntie, and Sister came back with me, Bob was already gone. We figured he would contact Dad to explain what had happened.

Meanwhile, in the building, Auntie and the officers kept arguing over her nationality. She seemed to have used that as a way of entertainment. She gave them a hard time, and when they had finally decided they would deport her to Honduras, she pulled out her identification and tossed it on the table.

I still remember the officer's reaction when she pulled it out. It was funny to notice she had been playing with them the whole time. Even I believed that she didn't have her ID. She smiled as she saw their angry faces and heard them say: "We have so much work, so many people and you made us waste a lot of time!"

"Well stop getting so many people! Let them get to their destination, and you won't have this many. Plus, that's your job anyway!" She answered sassily.

About an hour had already passed since they stopped us. I didn't see Amber around anymore. A different officer came to get us and walked us to a room. He stood at the door holding it open for us. When we got in, he shut it and locked us inside. It was different. I had never seen a room like it before. The walls were made from metal. It had nothing else, but a bench made of metal, and a toilet inside the same room that was covered with a small wall that only covered our private body parts. Of course, it too was made from metal.

We began trembling in no time. They had turned on the AC to what felt like the coldest temperature. We had no shoes on, no sweater, our hair and our underclothes were still wet, and the metal was making it feel even worse. We looked at each other's pale faces. My eyes were closing. I laid on the metal bench which felt warmer than the floor. I felt like I was in the North Pole. We were really being punished.

Auntie walked slowly to the door, and from the very small window, she asked one of the officers nicely to turn down the air conditioner a little. We waited, trying to get an answer from them. They turned it up even colder! I couldn't feel my hands. In fact, I couldn't feel my entire body.

No matter how hard Mom tried to give us heat, we didn't feel it. We trembled unstoppably and our noses began to run. Mom's face looked pale and worried, and my sister was not moving. Auntie was very mad. She got up and started knocking on the window. Officers walked nearby, but none of them stopped. They ignored Auntie completely.

She started kicking the door and making a lot of noise. She didn't stop until one of the officers came and finally opened the door.

"What do you want?" he asked angrily.

"Turn off the air conditioner! It's very cold! Look at the girls! You are going to kill us!" She yelled at him even angrier.

"Can't do anything! The air conditioner is directed, and we don't have access to move the temperature up or down!" he said shutting the door again. Auntie kicked the door after him.

"You bunch of heartless people!" she yelled beginning to cry.

When she finally gave up, she came back to the bench and helped Mom warm us up. She hugged me, rubbed my hands, arms, and legs, and massaged me. She tried anything to give me some heat. I didn't really feel a thing. I felt like if my bones were frozen and they were hurting a lot. The AC was about the same temperature of a freezer, or at least that's how cold it felt. I fell asleep quickly. I felt very tired and weak. I was worried about Mom and Auntie. They gave us heat, but nobody gave them any.

That same night, immigration put another lady in the same room with us. Another immigrant with fallen dreams. She was from El Salvador. She came from a place much farther away from us. The moment she got in, she ran to feel my sister and me.

"Oh my God! They are very pale!" she said very worriedly.

"It's the temperature of the AC!" I heard Mom say weakly. She rubbed her hands together and put them on my face trying to give some warmness. Seeing that I wasn't responding, she stood up and started yelling at the agents to turn off the AC.

"It's useless!" Auntie told her without moving. "I already tried that. They only ignored me!"

"Somebody will have to listen!" she said. She started screaming very loudly. The officers just looked at her from the outside and kept walking.

THE STORY OF A DREAMER

"Open the door!" she yelled to them as she kicked it. She got no answer from them. It seemed as if we were invisible. Nobody stopped to see if we were fine. "You are killing people! You are the criminals, not us!" she screamed furiously. She was just trying to help us.

"If you don't want to listen, I will make you listen!" she murmured hitting the window. She looked around trying to find something to break it, but there was nothing. She used her own hands to punch the window many times. It was not easy to break, it was not thin; she didn't care. I bet her fist was hurting a lot and I had no doubt that she was going to feel pain and have bruises for the next couple of days.

Auntie was very weak, but she somehow got the strength to stand up and help her. They both hit the window many times making it crack. It was then that the officers paid attention to them and after a serious argument between them, they finally turned off the AC.

It took us a while to recover in the room. I still felt very cold even with the AC off. I couldn't stop trembling.

Martha, the lady inside the room with us took her sweater off and covered my sister with it. We were in the room with her for about 3 hours. It was more than enough time to get to know her very well. She was a lovely, kind-hearted person. She worried a lot about us and didn't stop smiling even in the situation we were in.

Her story was painful. She was a strong woman. Her husband had taken her 2 little girls without her permission and brought them to the U.S. She was crossing the border to see them again. She cried as she told Mom about them. My heart melted as I listened and cried along.

It had been exactly 20 days since she had left her home to come to the U.S. It was heartbreaking to see good people like her suffer so much. Her story inspired me to one day share my own story with the world and to become somebody someday and show all those people what I wanted to come to this country for. I thank God for sending Martha our way because if she hadn't entered that room, I don't know if I would still be alive.

Very early in the morning the following day, one of the officers came to get us all out of the room. They separated Martha from us. Everything happened so quickly that we didn't even get a chance to say good-bye or thank her, for the last time. I just hope with all my heart that she got to see her daughters again. People like her, don't deserve to suffer as much. I have no doubt that wherever she is, God will pay her back for helping us.

Chapter

XXV

*I*t was around 3 am the next day when they took us to court. It was us, and 3 other people in the van. On our way, they talked about how they had been caught. Each one of them intended to have a good life in the U.S. They wanted to work, to have their own businesses, and to support their families. They didn't want to harm or destroy the country. They were good people who wanted to succeed. "But I will try again," one of them said, "I haven't given up yet."

During our silence, we pondered and worried about what would happen next. I was very afraid that they could put us, or at least Mom, in jail. When we finally got to court, the officer opened the back door of the van and took down the gates they had between the door and us. They instructed us to get out one by one. Three more officers waited outside for us to go in.

The court was about half the size of the other building; it was very small. There were rooms just like the one they had put us in with smaller windows. It was about the right size to put one head there. Dozens of immigrants stood, kneeled, or sat quietly on the floor. As we waited our turn, the officers passed out to each immigrant bread and milk as breakfast. It was not enough, but it was better than nothing.

Everyone ate without saying a word. People asked Mom a question or two about my sister and me but avoided having a whole conversation. They seemed afraid, and we were too. When our time arrived, they took each one of us to a machine and made us put our fingerprints of all ten fingers on both hands. They made Mom sign lots of documents and took pictures of her.

The same process was repeated with Auntie. When they took our information and warned us, they took us back to the van which drove for a couple minutes and the next time the gates opened, we were back on the Mexican side of the border.

"Get out!" the agent called holding the door open and setting us free. People looked at us as we walked barefooted. We were back worse than before. Without money, without clean clothes, without shoes without anyone to help us. We didn't know anyone.

We never heard from Bob again, and neither did Dad. He never told my dad we had been caught. He took the money my dad had given him and never went back to work with him again. I just hope from the bottom of my heart that he is okay enjoying what he has. Our first adventure went very bad. We lost almost everything we had. But I will never regret the experience. We were thrown back to Mexico without one cent in our pockets. But I wasn't afraid anymore. I knew God was with us. He was the whole time. We might have been broke, but we were not broken.

Chapter

XXVI

or the next week, we stayed in the same hotel we had stayed at before. Mary, our friend from the restaurant, introduced us to a new coyote she knew. She talked very highly of him. He went to the restaurant frequently and sometimes brought some of his people with him. She had heard from clients that they were all very nice and respectful. They took good care of the people when crossing the border.

One day, the coyote and Mom had a long conversation. He did seem to be a very nice person. He talked to Mom very respectfully and positive. Mom told him about what had happened to us the week before. He felt very sorry for us. He told Mom he wanted to help us get to the other side. He even offered his house for us to stay so we didn't have to pay for a hotel.

I was so not ready to cross the border once again. He came around to look for Mom every day until she accepted his help. We stayed in his house for about 3 weeks before crossing the border again. He was married, but his wife was on vacation visiting her parents, so he was alone in the house. During the time we stayed with him, his attitude did not change at all. He was as nice and respectful as he had been the first day. He treated us very well. He used to buy a lot of food and offered us everything without asking for one cent.

As a way of helping, Mom cooked for him and the whole crew daily. They were in love with her dishes. Every day she cooked something different. They all sat at the table ready, even before the food had finished cooking. They sniffed the food and ate as if they hadn't eaten in years.

The rest of the crew were as nice as Cesar, the coyote who had brought us there. Their main boss "El Gato" as they called him, walked on crutches. His left leg had been shot by immigration a couple months before. He seemed to have adapted. He moved from one place to another easily.

El gato had an older brother who was even nicer. He was my favorite of all. He was also one of the coyotes that walked with people to cross the border. They all had a schedule. Not the same coyotes walked every trip. They took turns. I remember El gato's brother came to see us every day at the house. He played with me for a little, while Mom cooked.

"Chucas," as they called him stole my little heart very fast. My innocent eyes saw him as a great human being. In no time, I began calling him "uncle." He had such a great heart that I wanted him to be part of my family. I missed him when he wasn't around. I heard immigration had caught him a few times. That meant that he was very close to going to jail. I worried when he made a trip. He was not a criminal. He was such a good person that did not deserve to go to jail.

One day, while he played with me, I asked him to be the person to cross the border with us. I trusted him more than any other coyote. He promised me, crossing his heart, that he would do it. "No voy a dejar sola a mi sobrina!" he would say.

At first, I thought all the coyotes were mean. That all they cared about was the money. But these people had totally changed my opinion. I felt very lucky to have such a great relationship with all of them. The way they treated me, made me want to stay there forever. I was so happy to be there that I forgot the reason we were there in the first place. Chucas spoiled me very much. He would bring a different fruit every day for my sister and me. She liked him as well, but he was closer to me.

I remember the day I got mad at him for not wanting to marry my aunt. I walked outside to the patio avoiding seeing him and started sweeping the dry leaves on the floor. He stood in the kitchen talking to Mom for a while and then came outside with me. He held the dustpan for me and meanwhile, he spoke to me with the softest voice I could have ever heard. "Perdoname por no casarme con tu tia pero... Nisiquiera la conozco!" he said, sadly. My aunt I wanted him to marry was my mom's younger sister who lived in Chiapas. And he was right, he hadn't even seen her in a picture. But I was too young to understand.

I will never forget the way he spoke to me that day. He did a lot of things to try to gain my forgiveness. I was very hard on him. He sat with me at the table quietly. Trying to get me to talk to him again. He took a napkin and a pen, and when it was time for him to make another trip, he said: "No te enojes! Mira, te voy a dar mi nombre y numero de telefono para que no me olvides." I still have that napkin. I brought it with me all the way from Mexico. It might be just a napkin, but for me, it is one of the most precious gifts I received in my life. Coming from a person that I will never, ever forget.

Chapter

XXVII

*I*t was close to the end of the year when our second try at crossing the border began. December 24, 2004, to be exact; Christmas eve. As he had promised, my uncle Chucas was leading the group. About twenty-five people came with us on that trip besides the two coyotes. "I won't abandon you!" he reminded me as I got nervously inside the car which would take us to the Rio Grande.

Part of my mind told me not to trust him completely; after all, he was a coyote. But my heart believed and trusted him with no doubt. With my Lord's blessing, I got in the car hoping that this time, we got to see my dad. We were all nervous. The coyotes looked the same way. Both had been caught before and were at risk of going to jail.

The youngest coyote was about 26 years old. Another coyote jumped in the truck to be the one dropping us off. Unlike the old man, they took the highway with all those people aboard to lead us to the Rio Grande. Behind the truck, a small car followed with El gato and two more coyotes aboard. They wanted to make sure we got to the river safely and soundly. They put all the other immigrants on the back of the truck laying down but kept my mom, Auntie, Sister, and I in the front.

The night was very cold. My sister and I were the only children on that trip. And the people totally understood why they kept us inside. We sat in complete silence waiting to get there. The truck drove for about fifteen minutes and then stopped on the side of a lonely highway.

"Salgan rapido!" the driver instructed all of us. Chucas quickly stepped out and helped us get out as the other coyote helped the people in the back. He took my and my sister's hands and started walking toward the trees. All the people followed him as our way started getting darker and darker. Mom and Auntie walked right behind us. We walked for about thirty minutes to get to the river; getting our eyes trained to the dark.

Chucas didn't let our hands go at any time. He walked quietly at a reasonable pace to make sure we were fine. The coyotes began crossing people to the other side of the river as soon they saw water. They used the same kind of buoyancy donuts the old man had used. But they did not have enough for everyone. We had to take turns. The immigrants that knew how to swim swam all the way to the other side of the river. It was much easier for me to go into the river this time. It was dark, and I couldn't see anything else besides the reflection of the water.

My uncle Chucas held my hand tightly as I entered the river toward the donut that he was holding for us. The water was just as cold as it had been the very first time we crossed, but the wind felt much colder. I waited in the water as Chucas stretched his hand to my sister trying to help her come next. Her fear of the river soon started to show. She started crying and begging Mom to go back. "No pasa nada!" El gato said as he came out from the trees. I was surprised, wondering how on earth he had gotten there if he only had one leg and 2 crutches! "Agarra su mano y no te muevas!" he demanded.

She started crying even harder. The immigrants stared at her. I know it was hard, but she was starting to make me mad. If she kept crying the way she was, we were all going to get caught. I knew all the people around her were thinking the same thing; we were worried. "Vamos! Date prisa! Tenemos los minutos contados!" El gato started pushing her.

She refused to take my uncle's hand. Mom had no other option than to scold her. That made her cry even more. So Chucas grabbed her hand against her will and pulled her into the water. I was totally convinced he didn't want to hurt her or even make her cry even more, but it was not only her; there were twenty-five more people wanting to get to the United States. "Vas a estar bien, te lo prometo. Pero por favor deja de llorar" he whispered to her as he put her on the floating donut with me.

Chucas protected us more than himself in the water and the whole way. He swam all the way to the other side of the river pulling the 2 donuts. I saw El Gato disappear as we got closer to the other side. People waited anxiously on both sides of the river. I admired Chucas and the other coyote for crossing that river so many times in one trip. I couldn't imagine myself crossing so often. Even though I loved water, I didn't like that river a bit.

My uncle got us to the other side of the river safely. He picked a spot and told us to wait for him there while he got the rest of the people through the river. We did as he told us to do and waited for him to get to us. From the other side, it didn't look that scary seeing the people cross the river. But I knew exactly how they felt. We never knew what could be under the water. It was not easy, but Chucas's attitude and calmness made everything look so simple. I thought about how much I would miss him when I got to the U.S. with Dad. He was a unique stranger who I did not want to lose.

On our side of the river, we could already hear immigration. We could also hear cars going from side to side. What surprised me more was the sound of dogs barking. I really didn't know where we were exactly. I couldn't see anything from my spot. I was curious to see where the sound of the dogs was coming from. "The dogs belong to the border patrol" I heard the other coyote explain to an immigrant. "They use them to sniff people and get them easily," he said.

I started questioning myself why we had to take this route if there were dogs there. It looked very easy for dogs to get people, especially a big group like us. We observed them quietly from the ground for a while as we tried to read which way they went.

Not too far away from the dark spot where we were hiding, I saw houses with lightbulbs outside which helped the border patrol have a good view of most of the land. There were many border patrol agents around. All of them had a dog. They began spreading out taking different routes. Each one also carried a hand lamp. Chucas watched them attentively, waiting for the first opportunity to get out of there. Still, on the ground, he once again took my hand and my sister's. When the closest agent turned around, he instructed everyone to run.

We all got up quickly on his command. Our pathway was still dark, but the lightbulbs helped a lot. Everything was trees and grass. We all ran in a single line trying to make the least noise possible. It didn't take too long for the dogs to spot us. They barked loudly in our direction as we threw ourselves to the ground once again. Chucas protected us by putting his arms around us once we were on the ground. No one moved. No one said a word. We all stared at the agent who walked with the dog leashed in our direction.

He seemed to know there were people around, but he didn't know where exactly. The dogs barked nonstop. Before they came too close to us, my uncle instructed that we run all the way to the wire wall which didn't seem too far from where we were.

Taking my sister's and my hand again, he began running very fast. The young coyote was up front. People tripped as they ran and fell to the ground. Noticing we were running away the agent unleashed the dog who ran angrily after us. I was very afraid. Dogs had always been one of my greatest fears. No matter how small or friendly they seemed, they always scared me. The one running behind us didn't look small or friendly at all. It looked a lot like a wolf.

He didn't stop barking which scared me even more. Aware of us, the rest of the agents unleashed their dogs as well. I heard nothing but dogs barking everywhere. They all ran after us as the agents did the same thing. Running out of breath, we finally hit the wire wall. Chucas quickly helped me and my sister climb up. I did my best to climb it as fast as I could and stopped once I got to the other side asking Chucas about my mom, who I didn't see.

"Continua! Sigue a los demas!" he yelled. "Yo ayudare a tu mama!" he promised.

I couldn't leave without seeing them get safely to the other side of the wire wall. The people ran after the younger coyote as they stepped on the other side of that wire. The dogs got closer and closer each second. Mom was one of the last people to make it to the wall. "Come on! come on, Doña!" Chucas rushed her desperately as he waited. He helped Mom get safely up the wire first, and as he gave his first step up, the closest dog got his leg in the air.

My heart stopped beating for a second. Mom stopped on the very top of the wire before getting to the other side. The dog bit his pants angrily. I stood there watching paralyzed. "Go! Leave me!" he yelled. He wanted us to continue without him. No matter how many people listened to him, I refused. With my hands shaking, I started picking up rocks and throwing them at the dog. Chucas was the only one still on that side of the wire; everyone else had crossed safely.

The rest of the dogs barked louder as they came closer. My fear was so immense that I began to cry. "If you don't come with me, I don't want to keep going!" I insisted as I kept throwing rocks at the dogs. Those were some the longest seconds of my life. "kick him, Uncle!" I yelled through my tears. He listened to me and kicked the dog, but the dog was strong and very well trained. One kick didn't even move him. Chucas kicked him several times before the other ones got there, and when the dog finally opened its mouth ready to take another bite, Chucas took a huge step up the wire. The dog jumped after him, but Chucas managed to escape safely.

By the time he got to the top of the wire wall, he had 6 more dogs after him, barking loudly and angrily. "Stop!" one of the agents yelled as he ran after us. Chucas took my hand, and we ran after the other people. My mind was so busy thinking about what had just happened that I didn't even notice if Mom was still with them or not. We followed the people who had entered in a neighborhood of very small houses. Each house had only one room.

The coyote went in the first house, and we all followed him. The plan was to make it to that house and wait for a van to pick us up. The small room became crowded. Inside, there was only a small bed that took up a large amount of space in the room. Chucas and the other coyote waited impatiently for all the people to get in. We were tired. We had run too much. When they were sure all the people were in the room safely, they started planning what would happen next.

As we stood quietly catching our breath, we saw my mom walking in the neighborhood. She looked fatigued; she could barely walk. Worst of all, she wasn't walking alone. A uniformed agent was helping her get to the house. He walked with no rush next to her. There were no other people outside besides them. He brought her to the house we were in, held the door open for her, and then locked all of us in.

We turned our attention to Mom as she entered the house calmly, waiting for an explanation. "He told me he was on our side. That he would bring me with you all!" She said sounding confused. According to her, the agent had lied saying that he had received a payment from the coyotes to let them cross the border. Mom believed him. The agent outside called more agents who got there with dog catchers' vans.

We waited inside the tiny house quietly. I felt terrible knowing that Chucas and the other coyote were going to jail this time. We all looked at each other sadly.

"Let's escape!" I heard the younger coyote propose to Chucas. "I am not going to jail!" he said.

"You have a plan?" Chucas answered.

"Listen, as soon as he comes back and opens the door we'll run nonstop!"

The rest of the people started freaking out when they heard them. "What? You guys are going to leave us here?" one of the immigrants asked. "And what do you want us to do? Spend the rest of our lives in jail?" the young coyote answered angrily.

Chucas turned to me very sad. "Go!" I told him. "I don't want to see my uncle in jail. He is not a criminal!". I saw him wipe his eyes. I knew his heart was breaking as well as mine.

"Thank you so much for everything, Chucas" Mom said reaching her hand toward him. "God will bless you for helping me and my daughters". He shook Mom's hand without saying a word. Everyone else stood in complete silence. The two coyotes hid behind the wall waiting for the door to be opened so they could escape.

Three border patrol vans arrived. An agent walked toward the house we were locked in and told the agent who had caught us: "Hey! Congratulations man! You just caught like 30 criminals by yourself. That doesn't happen often. When I grow up, I want to be like you!" he joked. They stood at the metal door watching us from the outside and smiling.

"Stupid Mexicans! You think you can come to our country anytime you want? You are not welcome!" he yelled kicking the door angrily.

Everyone trembled except the coyotes. His words made them furious.

"Enough John!" another agent yelled to him from behind. The younger coyote mumbled offenses against the white-skinned agent. His racist words had offended him.

Meanwhile, Chucas stood behind the door quietly and looking down. He didn't move. I knew he was nervous as he prepared to run away. This would be the last time I'd see him. The three agents walked toward the door. They talked to each other about how many people they would put in each van. One of them held the key to the door saying: "Okay people! One by one you are going to come out the door and tell me your complete name and where you are from."

"Click" we heard as the door was unlocked. My heart was pounding. I couldn't hold back my tears, and I didn't want to see what came next. I hid my head behind Mom closing my eyes tightly. Mom understood my sadness and hugged me.

It took the coyotes a few seconds to get the action started. I closed my eyes tightly, but I heard as they pushed the door open forcefully and started running. "Hey! Stop! Freeze!" I heard the agents yell. My attention instantly turned to what was happening outside as I heard a gunshot. I dropped to the floor. I couldn't feel anything; I couldn't even cry. It was as if I were dead for a minute. The only thing I could think of at that moment was Chucas. I imagined the worst when I heard that gunshot. I didn't want to believe immigration had gone that far.

Mom and some of the other people picked me up off the floor and started blowing to give me some air. I felt very strange. I had never felt that way before. It was hard to explain, but I didn't want to live anymore. My entire body felt weak, and my chest was full of tears that I was trying to get out but couldn't.

I closed my eyes for a minute, and when I opened them again, Chucas was right there beside me.

"Didn't I tell you I would be with you until the end?" he said. "This is not over yet. You still need me."

Chapter

XXVIII

*A*s they put us in the vans, we were separated from everyone else; including Auntie. The immigration agent driving was super nice compared to the rest. He looked Hispanic, spoke perfect Spanish and he was very young. Mom talked to him as he drove us to the court. She tried to convince him to set us free. "Dejenos aqui, le prometo que no diremos nada" she begged. He smiled and moved his head side to side.

"I'm sorry ma'am! I really can't do that. That's breaking the rules!" He explained nicely. "One has already escaped, and we will get in serious trouble for it."

We all saw the young coyote's shoe stuck on one of the wires as we drove by. "Look at that! Cinderello lost his shoe!" he joked with us as he picked up his radio to announce to his teammates. The young agent took us to the same court that they had taken us to the first time. Once we were there, we were reunited with Auntie, Chucas, and the rest of the people.

Chucas seemed sad as he entered the crowded court holding my hand. We stood in front of other people as there weren't any seats or space on the walls where we could lean. As they began taking people's information, another agent came around and fed the immigrants a biscuit big enough for two bites and an orange juice that tasted very disgusting.

We were all so hungry that everyone except my sister accepted the food gratefully. She was very mad. She left the agent with his hand stretched and refused to take the food.

"No gracias, no tengo hambre!" she said without looking at him.

"You have to take it!" the agent insisted.

"No quiero nada!" she answered with an angry tone of voice.

Another agent sitting right in front, stared at her, and asked, "Are you mad?"

"Yes!" she replied.

"Here, eat it!" the agent insisted angrily.

"Te dije que no quiero nada!" she answered rudely.

Chucas quietly interrupted the argument and told the agent nicely: "Please give it to me, she is not hungry right now, but I will hold it for her until she gets hungry."

The agent did as Chucas asked and walked away unhappily. Uncle Chucas was nice enough to keep the biscuit in the pocket of his sweater and fed it to my sister later.

Meanwhile, the rest of the agents interviewing my sister gave her a hard time asking: "Are you angry?" She looked at them furiously without saying a word.

"She is mad because we caught her" the agent next to him said, laughing.

Only the agents thought it was funny. Honestly, I thought it was funny too. Of course, it made me mad that they were laughing at us as immigrants, but I couldn't deny they were doing a great job of making my sister mad and giving her a hard time. They laughed hardly as the rest of the immigrants stared at them angrily. They felt superior to us just because they were wearing their uniforms, but I knew that no matter what position you are in, there is always someone above you.

As I looked around, I noticed a big crowd of people from Central America. They were getting themselves ready to go back to their country. Many of them cried silently. Others watched from behind bars. In our spot, we trembled as we signed our deportation documents. I felt even worse when I looked at Chucas and remembered he wasn't coming back home with us. I stared at him trying to memorize every single movement that happened at the moment of his arrest.

The agent with him did not say a word. As soon as he finished entering Chucas's information into the system, he looked behind him, and without saying anything, he snapped his fingers and pointed to him instructing two other agents to arrest him. The two agents made him kneel, put the handcuffs around his wrists, and pushed him toward the jail. They treated him like a criminal when all he had really done was protect us.

No matter how hard he tried, he couldn't hold his tears back anymore. He began crying quietly looking down. I started crying hard as all my emotions flooded to the surface. I couldn't control myself. I walked toward him and begged the agents to set him free. It felt like if he was about to get killed.

Everyone watched as I got on my knees and cried nonstop. "Mi tio no!" I wailed. All eyes were focused on me. The moment became more intense as another immigrant knelt next to me and tried to lift me up.

The noise and screams caught the attention of the rest of the agents working inside the other offices. They began coming out of their offices, one by one. The two agents holding Chucas were not the exception when it came to being moved by the emotion of the moment. They both held one of his arms and allowed me to hug him for the last time. Mom, Sister, and Auntie sobbed too but did not come near me.

"What is going on here?" I heard a deep voice ask behind me.

I continued crying without looking back. Chucas was the only thing I cared about at that moment. As one the agents ran to whom appeared to be their boss, I turned around slowly and noticed an old, American man standing behind the front desk saying, "You again, young man? Didn't I warn you last time that if I catch you again, I will put you in jail?" he asked Chucas sternly.

"Yes, sir!" Uncle Chucas answered politely still looking down.

"What are you doing here, then? Do you want to spend the rest of your life behind bars?" he asked.

Chucas did not say a word. Inside his and my eyes, the storm continued. I began crying even harder as another immigrant woman walked up to me and wiped away my tears. I leaned on her shoulder for a couple seconds and then turned and noticed that the old agent was staring at me. He looked at me for a couple of seconds and then told my uncle: "I am going to give you one more chance, but I don't want to see you here ever again, understood?"

We were thrown back to Mexican territories once again. This time, though, I felt protected. The angel they called Chucas had demonstrated me that I could trust him and showed me what a big heart he had. As the years pass, my love and appreciation for him remain the same. I might have had forgotten a little about his appearance, but I will never, ever forget his name and the kind human being that God put in my path.

Chapter

XXIX

*I*t took only a couple days to find our next coyote. In fact, it was Chucas who recommended him. After the last two fails, the last thing my sister and I wanted was to try again. We wanted to go back to Chiapas, and we told Mom about it. She knew it was causing us a trauma. We were too little to be experiencing all these things.

In a broken voice, she sat and talked to us one Saturday morning as she pleaded, "Please, just one last try. If they catch us again, I swear I will send you back with your grandma, and I will try by myself." She had promised she would do that before the last attempt. Now, she was asking for one last chance.

Before we left Cesar's house, I asked Chucas to promise me he was not going to risk his life again. "Remember, if they catch you, they will put you in jail," I reminded him. He hugged me tightly as he responded "I can't promise you I won't cross the border again because I would be lying to you. This is my job, we must take risks. But I can promise you I will be more careful and run for my life." He said smiling as he crossed his heart. "And I also promise I will come visit you!".

That promise turned my frown upside down. I was happy to know that I would see him again for sure. I wished he could have been the one to cross the border with us again, but he refused to do it. He wouldn't explain why when we asked. Deep in my heart, I knew he didn't want to see us suffer any more.

"Take good care of them. They are special to me!" I heard him tell "Bailas", the new coyote he introduced us to.

They seemed to have a good relationship. Chucas told us they had known each other for years. Bailas had a huge house. He had many coyotes working for him. He even had his own cook whom they called "El Diablo."

Everyone was very friendly. Bailas treated us very well. He gave us a room to stay in.

In the living room, he had many immigrants waiting to cross the border. The refrigerator was always loaded with a lot of food. He reminded every immigrant who came to his house that they could eat anything from the kitchen. Every day el diablo cooked for the whole house. His food was delicious! The dining room wasn't big enough to fit everybody, so all the immigrants got their plates and ate in their own spots.

Bailas had a little girl of about five-years-old. She came to the house frequently, but she did not live there. She lived with her mom who was separated from Bailas. I got along with the coyotes easily, especially with the younger ones. I liked all of them, but none of them was as special as my uncle Chucas. The closest one to me was "Catracho". He was the youngest of all at 20 years old, he liked to mess with me a lot. He played pranks on me all day long when he was around. He was always laughing, and he was very respectful as well. He did the same job as Chucas but unlike him, Catracho had never been caught.

Catracho was also the one who would help me clean the patio every now and then. That was one of my favorite things to do since we couldn't do much else. I loved to put the dry leaves together. Catracho enjoyed making me mad by spreading the leaves all over the place again once I had them together. It pissed me off sometimes, but I couldn't help laughing. He was just too funny to stay mad at for long.

Every day, I saw new faces in the living room. It was getting crowded. Among the immigrants staying in the house was a young guy from Honduras whose name was Alex. Alex was very quiet and very nice. He told Mom about his experience crossing the first border. He had really suffered. It was way more difficult for them because they not only had to cross the border between Mexico and the USA, but they also had to cross the border between Central America and Mexico.

His story was very depressing. He had been rejected by both of his parents. They didn't even notice that he was not in Honduras anymore. He rode the train to the Mexican border. "I saw people die as they tried to get on the train when it was moving," he told Mom the night we met him. "I was able to help a few people get on the train safely, but there were just too many, and I couldn't help everybody. Believe it or not, there are even kids riding that dangerous transportation."

It was heartbreaking to hear that, I knew I wasn't suffering as much compared to them. His words made me realize many things, including how lucky I was to have been born in Mexico.

Alex taught me not to complain about what was happening to me. His story made me feel more grateful to God because, despite all we had suffered, my whole body was complete. Alex told us that he'd seen a man's leg cut off as he tried to get on a train.

Chapter

XXX

*O*ur days flew by in that house. I enjoyed listening to the stories of the immigrants coming into the house. I grew close to some people so when their time to leave came, I felt depressed. There were days when I felt sad and didn't know why. I stayed in bed and told Mom I wanted to sleep some more so that she couldn't notice my depression.

I had so many things on my mind. I remembered the people I had met over the last couple of months and how life had separated me from them. Uncle Chucas was always my main worry. Not knowing what was happening with him was tough. I didn't even know if he was still free or not. I asked Mom constantly about him, but she knew nothing about him either. I also wondered if the people I met in the living room had ever made it to the other side.

New Year's was around the corner. It marked another year without seeing my father. I knew it was as hard for him to be a country away from us as it was for us to be away from him. We constantly talked on the phone, but at a certain point talking to him depressed me even more. I didn't know what to expect of life anymore. I didn't know if it was even worth it to keep trying to get to the U.S.

I often sat in the corner of the living room looking at all the people who were risking their lives for a better future. I prayed to God and asked Him to make their lives less painful. I asked Him with all my heart to give me a chance one day to help all the good immigrants like the ones sitting around me. But I was just an eleven-year-old girl. What could I do to help?

Alex became so close to us that he called us his "hermanitas" and he referred to Mom as "mama." My mom liked him a lot, and so did we. He asked Bailas if he could wait for the trip until we were ready. He didn't want to be separated from us. I remember when we fought over which cartoon to watch on the TV. He spent most of the time in the room with us watching TV since there were only two in the house.

We made up a rule that was kind of stupid. The three of us liked different cartoons, and they all came on at the same time. Our rule was, "we get to watch all three cartoons for ten minutes each!" It was dumb because we didn't even understand what was going on in the episodes, but we always had a great time together.

Auntie was the only person who had a problem with Alex. They argued every time they saw each other. Their arguments were funny, and I think they just liked each other. Both ended up laughing after every argument, which is how I knew their arguments weren't serious.

New Year's Eve was a sea of tears. Everyone cried as they called their loved ones, including Mom. She cried as she talked to Grandma over the phone. It was her fifth New Year's away from them. I was getting used to seeing her cry every single New Year's, but that night, I totally understood what it felt like to be far away from a person you love so much.

Auntie cried as she talked to the daughters who she had left in Chiapas promising them a better future. I did not even know she had daughters until that night. I couldn't imagine how she was feeling.

Alex, as usual, cheered everyone up. He wasn't very good at communicating with words, but he gave the warmest hugs. The cook made piles of food for everyone in the house. Bailas and his crew didn't sit still until they got every single immigrant out to join them for dinner. I followed them against my will, but once everyone got distracted, I went back to the dark room and let my tears come out. I cried so much that I could feel my eyes so swollen and my head pounding in pain.

I couldn't understand why I was crying so much and why there was so much on my mind since I was just a little girl. I was very hungry, but I did not want to get out of bed. I didn't feel like doing anything or talking to anyone. Mom came in unexpectedly and heard me crying. I didn't have time to pretend I was sleeping.

"Que pasa?" she asked as she began stroking my hair. I didn't say a word to her.

"No me quieres decir?" she asked.

I hid my head and kept crying quietly under my pillow. "I think I know a person who you would be willing to talk to," she whispered as she left the room.

I was annoyed. The last thing I wanted was people around me. I had convinced myself that I hated everyone. I wanted to be alone, and she didn't seem to understand that.

A few minutes later, I heard the door open once again, and a shadow was at the door. I glanced at the door and cried even harder when I saw Chucas standing there. He ran and gave me a huge hug and kissed my cheek.

"Hey, happy New Year's!" he said wiping off my tears. "I promised you I would come back to see you, and here I am!" He said as he kept his arms around me.

At that moment, he was the only person in the world who could have cheered me up. He was also the last person I expected to walk in the room. His presence that night erased all my sadness. I considered him my best friend although I can't say I understand what made him so special to me.

That was the last time I saw my uncle Chucas. I am so grateful that God gave me that last chance to hug him tightly. He ate dinner with me in the bedroom that night. He chose to stay with me rather than going out to the party. It meant a lot to me. We had a long conversation. As I cried, he put my heart back together with his words. "One day, you will make it to the other side, and once you get there, I want you to work hard to be successful. God put you on earth for that reason, and I can see it in you. You will succeed in life. Just don't forget where you came from."

Since that day, I have taken his advice seriously and worked hard. I try to give the best of me every day. My goal every day is to do something productive that will lead me to success. At the end of the day, I like to feel like I deserve to go to sleep, and despite all the time I wasted doing nothing, I can always start from where I am.

Chapter

XXXI

"*L*isten carefully, idiots, these two** women, and the little girls are your main priority on this trip. If I hear you guys did something to them or abandoned them in the middle of the desert, I will rip your heads off. And you know I mean it!" Bailas warned the coyotes on the night we embarked on our third trip.

They nodded, looking thoughtful and serious. I could tell they were scared of him. Bailas always carried a gun with him, and as he talked to them, he would put his hand on it to make sure they understood he was serious. It was the first trip of the year. The trucks were loaded with about sixty-five people aboard. Five of them were coyotes, including El Diablo; the cook who had offered to join this trip to help Mom.

El Diablo was a very strong man for his age. He crossed the border and came back anytime he wanted. He had never been caught on any of the seven trips he had made. It was interesting to hear him say he would come back the same day he got to the other side. He had no intention of living in the U.S. He loved his job as a cook, and that was the only place where he was happy.

Alex kept his promise to stick with us from the moment we got on the truck that would take us to the river. I was way more nervous than the previous times for some reason. I was afraid I would fail again. Mom, Auntie, Sister, El Diablo, Alex, and Catracho laid with me in the back of the truck. I looked at the very last person laid at the end of the truck and began to imagine the worst. I bit my nails as I imagined that back door opening as the truck was in motion. I knew that the poor man was worried about the same. But there was no choice; somebody had to take that spot.

Catracho explained their plan to us as we waited for the truck to start. "From here, we are driving to the Rio Grande. We will walk all night and hopefully get to the other house very early in the morning. We might wait in that house a day or two and keep walking until we hit the border of Texas."

They had done the same thing many times. They knew which way to walk, the approximate time they would get there, and where the border patrols in that area were located.

At that point, I didn't care if I had to walk for five or six hours again. I was willing to walk and cross the river again without complaining. The only thing I didn't want was to land in immigration's hands one more time.

The trucks began moving slowly. One after another. We felt the freezing air more intensely as the truck drove faster. I didn't close my eyes at any time. I looked at the beautiful stars that the sky offered that night. The back of the truck was very uncomfortable and cold. Our heads jumped up and down like ping-pong balls as the truck accelerated. We all received painful bumps on the head. I didn't like it, and we had barely started.

Nobody moved from their spot. We were in positions where we couldn't even stretch. We were not even allowed to raise our heads. I saw the reflection of red traffic lights as the coyotes drove fast through them. Catracho said it was a twenty-five-minute drive to get to the river. I didn't hear too many cars on the road. It was lonely. The Coyotes drove faster and faster. They were trying to decrease the chances of the police catching them with all those people aboard.

But I guess it wasn't our lucky day. The speeding caught a cop's attention who was hidden on a valley near the road and instantly turned the sirens on. He drove right behind us. The rest of the trucks were gone. His bright emergency lights and the loud sirens drove all of us crazy.

We felt the truck slow down and stop. We all prayed as our hearts pounded loudly. I was so scared that I began running out of breath. No one said a word or even attempted to see what was happening. We felt a mini heart attack at every step the cop took towards the truck. But the coyotes had a plan—another illegal plan.

As soon as the cop hit the truck, they accelerated and drove off very fast. I felt my pulse pounding throughout my body. My fear was making my sense of hearing go on and off. I closed my eyes tightly and prayed. The Coyotes drove as if they had potatoes instead of people in the back of the truck. They made abrupt turns, which made some people roll out of their places and fall on top of each other.

Mom held my hand tightly while Alex held my other one trying to keep me from falling out of my place. My fear turned to tears. I felt I wasn't going to make it. Either the truck would crash, or a heart attack would kill me. I was that afraid.

The cop drove after us with the sirens still on. Unlike the coyotes, the cop slowed down as he made the turns and eventually was left behind. We were then taken to a dark valley that led to a farm.

"Bajense, rapido!" the driver shouted. We all got out of the truck having no idea where we were. As soon as the last person got out, the coyote drove off. Catracho held the barbed wires for everyone to hide on the farm. We were surrounded by cows and their excrement everywhere. It was not a fun place to be, but it felt much better than being on the truck.

We waited there for several minutes. The coyotes driving the truck were in contact with Catracho who, besides el diablo, was the only coyote with us. It was a stinky place to be hidden. Even though it was dark, we could see the glow of the excrement. It was kind of cool to be so close to the cows. I hadn't been that close to one since we had moved from Chiapas. At the same time, I was scared that they would step on us.

We were getting desperate and sleepy; mostly sleepy. I didn't really care if the truck came back or not. In fact, I was hoping it didn't. I laid on the cleanest spot I found and stared at the sky. I never noticed how beautiful the stars were until that night. Each one sparkled differently.

I smiled to myself as I dreamed with my eyes open. It was like each star was telling me something different about my future. That night, I felt my eyes sparkle as brightly as those stars. They were filled with illusion, strength, and positiveness.

The feeling was indescribable. I couldn't stop smiling. It was the most peaceful moment I had had in a long time. I knew I was feeling the presence of God somehow. He was telling me to keep going and that there were good things for me ahead of this trip. He had a plan for me, and something told me that all this pain I was going through would be worth it.

Chapter

XXXII

*I*t took the truck a while to come back, which was enough time to be filled with energy and positive thoughts. As we headed to the river, I was picturing those stars. We moved quietly and quickly. The bright moon lit our way as we walked down a dark pathway. El Diablo, Alex, and Catracho were always behind us. As they had said would be the case, we walked for about twenty-five minutes to get to the river. This time, the river crossing would be much riskier because the river was lit with very bright lights where we would cross it.

We hid behind huge rocks on the side of the river as the coyotes spied on immigration and watched for the right moment to proceed. The river sounded louder than ever. There was an arched bridge across the river. It was from there that the lights came. Under the bridge, there were some gigantic doors where water was coming from.

As the coyotes began giving us instructions, it wasn't making any sense to me. "First of all, you have to know that those offices on the bridge are immigration's. We are going to cross the river right in front of them. The doors under the bridge, are full of water. If for some reason, immigration notices us as we cross the river, they will open those doors and release a large amount of water, which could easily sink us. Something else, we don't carry floating donuts. We will cross the river altogether holding hands until the first person makes it to the other side of the river."

People looked at each other very confused. "Why would they bring us right in front of immigration if we are running away from them?" I heard people whisper. Besides the coyotes, no one thought it was a good idea. But it was too late to turn back. In the name of Christ, we all stepped into the river at the coyote's signal.

My sister didn't have enough time to hesitate as she had previously done, but she did cry as she walked into the water. Every single person on that trip mumbled a prayer as they entered the freezing water. The doors were our main fear. The water behind them was getting louder and louder. It was as loud as a strong storm. Before submerging in the water completely, the coyotes warned us that we would be stepping on rocks inside the river. "They are very pointy and cut easily, so I recommend leaving your shoes on."

Catracho was the first one to get in the water. He started pulling people as stood and indicated they were ready. Mostly the men were ready first. We watched nervously as each reached for the next person. No one was ready to go in, but we didn't have much time. We needed to do it quickly.

"Right now, we are a family," another coyote said to motivate the people still on dry land. "We need to help each other. Nothing is going to happen! We will make it to the other side safely!"

It was not until Alex joined the chain that we were brave enough to join too. Mom stood up after him and stretched her left hand to hold the next person who was my sister. She walked in crying quietly. As she grabbed Mom's hand, she reached the other one toward me. Each person who joined the chain meant we were a step closer to the other side. Catracho was already halfway there when my sister got into the water. I reached for her hand when el diablo interrupted, "No, I go first! If something happens, you won't be able to hold her weight!" he explained.

I joined the chain right after him and held his hand tightly. I could hear some people regretting not listening to the coyotes' advice about not taking their shoes off. The strong, powerful water moved our bodies back and forth. It was hard to stand still and even harder to advance quickly. It felt like rocks underneath the water had been put there on purpose to hurt people or make them trip. They were all on different levels, sizes and shapes. It was hard to guess what the next rock would be like. Some were pointy, others were slippery, and we came across some huge ones too as well as some spots where there were none.

The huge, bright bulbs hurt our eyes. We stared at them while we advanced. The water level reached my shoulders in no time. To my left, Auntie, as well as other people, prayed continuously. She held my hand tightly as we moved.

The angry water seemed stronger with every wave. It was so cold that we could see our breath in the air. Our cheeks felt frozen. I joined Auntie and started praying as I saw the last person enter the water. My heart was beating faster and faster. There were sixty-five souls on the water trying to get to the other side with no protection at all. All were at risk of being shot, drowning, or freezing. Even sixty-five people were not enough to reach from one side of the river to the other.

Mom kept her eye on us. That the doors would be opened was what I feared most. I couldn't shake the thought that if those doors opened, even a little, we would all die. "Please God, keep their eyes shut" I begged, feeling afraid.

All our chins trembled. Our bodies grew colder and colder every second that we were in the water. At one point, I realized that the water was clean. That made me wonder where it was coming from. Why had it been so dirty the other two times?

No border patrol was seen or heard. Smiles appeared on our faces as we saw Catracho make it across safely and soundly.

He quickly helped people out the water as they reached the other side. The sense of urgency we felt about reaching the other side increased as we saw fewer and fewer people on the chain. People put on dry clothes as they stepped out. The tension in the water increased. Most of the people had got out of the water safely, including us.

There were only ten more people in the water when the unexpected happened. The second-last young lady on the chain slipped and fell. We watched the current drag her away taking with her the last man as well, who had no one else to help him. They never came out. They did not set foot on American soil.

Chapter

XXXIII

"*D*o you see those lights** there?" one of the coyotes asked. "That's our stopping point! That's the United States!" he said cheerfully. The moonlight revealed the smiles on people's faces.

"We will be there in two hours maximum!" one of the immigrants called.

"Easy walk!" another one shouted happily.

None of the women opened their mouths. We were still shocked about what we had all seen at the Rio Grande. We just watched and listened.

The lights didn't seem too far away. "That's why we don't carry food or water!" the coyote explained, "It's a very short distance!" Alex hugged me as we waited for the signal to begin walking. He knew I was more frightened than ever before. He was a gentleman. He worried about us even though we were not related. We were not even from the same country. It made no difference to him. His love was as pure as his whole heart.

We walked at the front of the group. Next to us, Alex and el diablo walked quietly. As Bailas had instructed, the rest of the coyotes kept an eye on us at all times. The ground we were walking on was nothing but dust. No trees, no grass, no rocks. We walked nonstop never losing sight of those lights. The moon became brighter as the sky became darker. The cold didn't feel so bad when we walked quickly. The only sounds we heard were our steps.

We walked faster as the frequency of the lightning bolts increased. Soon, we were in the middle of a big storm. It made the whole trip harder than we had expected it would be. The dust turned to mud which stuck to our shoes.

We had nowhere to run to protect ourselves from the scary thunder and the strong storm. The cold was worse than ever, and there was a strong, cold wind blowing against us as we walked. El diablo stopped every three minutes to scrape the mud off my shoes with his hands. It packed very quickly to the point that I could barely walk. It felt just as if I were wearing high heels.

People got sick. Most of the woman started sneezing, including Mom who had already started to weaken. The coyotes seemed nervous. Sick and weak people made the trip more complicated. The lights seemed to be getting farther away by the minute. We drank rain water as we walked. Our pace slowed.

All I wanted to do was lie on the ground and wait for my body to respond. It was around three in the morning when I started to feel sick. I felt cold, but I was sweating. My temperature felt higher than usual. I felt my eyes starting to shut slowly. Every woman was complaining. Some of those behind me were falling. The Coyotes' main concern was not being able to make our destination before the sun came out.

They explained to us that they guided themselves through those lights. If the sun came out, they wouldn't be able to see the lights, and we might get lost. We forced our bodies to keep moving and tried to convince ourselves that we were getting close even though it was not true.

The coyotes mumbled amongst themselves trying to figure out what to do. The men, including Alex and el diablo, helped the women walk. The rain didn't stop. Puddles of water were formed everywhere. Our clothes were soaked.

The sky eventually began to clear as the storm weakened for the first time in two hours. I saw some of the people drinking the dirty water that the storm had left in puddles. Thankfully, with the help of the Lord and everyone's effort, we reached those lights right on time.

We were close enough to them to avoid getting lost. It was exactly six a.m. The land was starting to look different. We walked across miles of planted vegetables and fruits. The entire area seemed to be plantation soil. "We are very close," the coyotes said, "the house is just around the corner." That was a complete lie, but I understood that he was trying to encourage people to keep going.

The day began cloudy and cold. We made it to the house at around nine in the morning. Most of us were in bad conditions. We were hurt, hungry, thirsty, sick, dirty and tired. The house was a one-bedroom house in which there were about eighty-seven more immigrants. The place was so tiny that we could barely move. Once we got to the house, nobody could leave. Even walking outside was prohibited.

No one except the coyotes knew exactly where we were. The rest of us were not even sure if we were in Mexico or already in U.S. territory. The house had only one small window in the only bedroom. We were located right in front of the road. The houses around looked as tiny as the one we were in. I wondered where we were. We had already crossed the Rio Grande, which is the line that divides Mexico and the United States, but why did our surroundings look so much like Mexico?

No one was allowed to call family members. It felt as if we had been kidnapped. Different people left and entered the house every two days. El diablo went back with Bailas the day after we arrived at the house.

There were two people in charge of everyone inside. They made sure nobody escaped, made a phone call, or got too loud. Unlike Ballas's house, this house didn't have enough food in the refrigerator to keep everyone's stomach full. The house didn't even have a stove. People's stomachs cried very often. We were all very hungry. My sister and I were the only kids in the house.

Three days later, Mom tried to contact Bailas. She had a hard time convincing those people to let her make that call, but at the end of the day, they felt bad for us since we were the only two children.

During the call, Mom begged Bailas to allow her to call Dad. It had been already five days since our last call with him. That was enough time for him to imagine that something else had happened to us. Bailas not only allowed us to talk to Dad but he also instructed their men to make sure we got the only bed in the house. Even from far away, he was still treating us in a special way. We knew he was putting himself in Mom's shoes and thinking, "What if that were me crossing the border with my daughter?"

The coyotes usually didn't keep the same people for more than one week in the house. They proceeded with the next step in the order in which they came. In fact, all the people who had walked with us that night were gone.

We stayed until Mom was fully recovered. Alex, who had so many chances to keep going, refused to go until we were ready. Despite all the bad things and hard circumstances, my worse memory was seeing those innocent people drown in the river. I wished with all my heart that both of them had survived and been caught by the border patrol, but the chances of that happened were slim. It was as if that horrible moment had been videotaped as it replayed in my memory all day long.

Mom and Auntie got along well with the people who came into the house and especially the women. They all had a different story to tell. Among those people, we met a group of young men who slept with us in the bedroom. There were six of them between the ages of eighteen and twenty-five years old.

They had the weirdest hairstyles I had seen in my short life. Surprisingly, out of the six of them, only one spoke Spanish. He explained to us that they came from Oaxaca, which is the neighbor state of Chiapas and that the other five people only spoke a dialect that they learned as they grew up. They were all part of an Indian tribe.

Mom, Alex, and Auntie were fascinated with them. I wondered how they planned to communicate with people in the U.S. if they couldn't even speak Spanish. Mom gave each one of them a nickname since their real names were so hard to pronounce. We made fun of each other as we talked. My favorite part was watching them wake up in the morning with their hair styles even more messed up. That was a blast!

Chapter

XXXIV

*B*y the time Mom recovered, we were already used to the house. It was getting harder and harder to accept that we would be walking a long distance again soon. Honestly, I didn't want to continue. We had heard about the experience from some of the immigrants who had used Bailas and his people to cross the border previously. They said things like, "Getting here is nothing compared to what is after this," or "From here on, we don't walk for hours; we do it for days!"

Their comments made the trip sound scarier than what we had imagined. When Mom called Dad, she told him all of that. Dad understood the danger and braveness we were showing, and he tried to encourage us saying, "Give it a try! You are halfway there! I invested all my money to see you and my daughters again. Please give me the opportunity."

I understood how desperate he was to have us back with him. However, Mom didn't see it that way. Dad's comment about the 'investment' led to an argument between the two them, to the point that Mom decided we were not going to continue. I was happy to know that I wouldn't have to walk anymore, but deep inside, it broke my heart to know I wouldn't see Dad again.

There were more people and less food every day in that small house. Alex had to 'steal' the food every night to feed us. He would hide some cookies, chips, and juice under our bed for the next day. Sometimes, if we were hungry, he would eat with us at midnight silently. I remember him arguing with Auntie for eating part of the food he had in store for us. "I brought this for my sisters! Not you!" he would say. It was so comical to hear them argue back and forth.

One middle January night while everyone slept, a loud voice came in the door. The entire house was dark. We only had a manual lamp as our light. As the person walked closer to the room, I could hear more than one voice. I couldn't really hear what they were saying, but they were talking to all the immigrants in the living room. I saw the reflection of a bright light as they pointed to different people. When they arrived in the bedroom, they turned the lamp on even brighter and said in a loud voice: "This is Immigration! Get up!"

Everyone sat shocked, staring at them right away. They moved the light slowly from left to right trying to get a count of how many people were in the house. I felt my heart drop to my stomach instantly. Everyone sat without saying a word.

"Show me your papers!" he demanded the closest woman. There was no answer or movement from her side. The woman began shaking as she slowly began putting her hands in the air.

He stood in front of her for a few seconds with the lamp pointing to her face and then let out a giggle saying: "Just kidding! I am a coyote!"

I didn't know if I should laugh or be mad. What he did was very serious. He could have easily given somebody a heart attack, but there was no doubt he nailed it. It was the best, worst prank I have had played on me. I was grateful that it led to nothing but laughter afterward.

That same week, in a group of people brought to the house, we met a young woman from Guatemala. She was the mother of a boy and a girl around the same ages as my sister and me. She told us everything they had been through. Her life had been tough, and she was a strong woman for coming from so far away with her kids. Just like Alex, she and her kids had to cross two borders to make it to the U.S. It had been exactly three weeks since she left her country with her kids in search of the American Dream.

All three of them seemed very tired and weak. She was worried about her kids. She showed us the broken soles of their shoes and said, "I don't know how my kids are going to keep walking with those shoes. Water, dirt, and rocks got inside their shoes and make it hard to walk on top of that, they were already torn. I wish my shoes were broken instead of theirs."

It broke our hearts to see those innocent kids suffering. When we heard that, my sister and I knew right away what to do. After getting Mom's approval, we took our shoes off and told them: "You can have our shoes! You still have a long way to go, and I bet these are a little more comfortable than the ones you are wearing!"

Their mom broke down in tears. The kids accepted the shoes gratefully. The mother hugged us tightly as Mom explained to her that we were not continuing but going back where we started. My heart felt happy to know that we had done the right thing. They left the house the next day. Like so many others we met, we never saw them again and had no idea if they made it to the other side.

Chapter

XXXV

*I*t was near the end of January when we saw Catracho again. He was surprised to see that we were still at the house. "What are you still doing here? Why haven't you advanced?" he asked Mom that afternoon, very confused.

"We are going back! We are not continuing!" Mom answered.

"Nobody goes back once you are here!" he said seriously. "What is the problem? Why don't you want to continue?" he asked.

"I don't have enough money to pay you guys to bring me to Texas!" she whispered to his ear.

Catracho looked at her seriously and said: "That is not a problem. We can fix that with a phone call!" He took his phone out and dialed as he walked away. A few minutes later, he walked in again and handed his phone to Mom saying, "the boss wants to talk to you!"

She took the call and talked to Bailas for about thirty minutes. During the call, Bailas pushed Mom forward saying: "I've known you enough and I know all you want is get to Dallas to be reunited with your husband. I've never done this for anyone, but I will make an exception for you. Go with tonight's group and don't worry about the money. I trust you. When you get to the United States, and you have it, you can send it to me."

Bailas did so much for us even from far away. He was giving Mom so much help that we had no more excuses to stay there. As she hung up the phone, she remembered we had given our shoes away. She told Catracho about it, and he replied: "I can get your girls some shoes, but we have to leave in one hour no matter what."

One hour was not enough time to get myself prepared. My heart was beating too fast as I put on my winter clothes. Catracho came back five minutes later with two pairs of shoes. They were both size six. The perfect size for my sister but one number too small for me.

That was all he could get, and there was no time to look for other shoes my size. Only I knew the shoes were not my size. I forced my feet into them. The socks I was wearing weren't necessarily the thinnest one, which made my shoes even more tight. Still, I did not say a word about it.

As Catracho had warned us, the trucks started driving right on time. Seventy immigrants besides the Coyotes, came aboard that night. Every single man carried a gallon of water, while the coyotes carried cans of food and tortillas. That seemed like a lot of food and water. We didn't know how long we were walking. We were hoping about the same distance we walked from the Rio Grande to the house.

The sky was already dark as we hit the spot that would be our starting point. We all stood still, praying, as the coyotes searched the area. The place was silent. Gigantic trees lined each side of the pathway. There was no light at all besides the moon.

"It is going to be a long way, but we will get to the other side for sure!" one of the coyotes said. I didn't know if that was good or bad news. They told us they had always used the same path and had never been caught. "There is no border patrol here! So, we can take rests when you all feel tired" he offered. "Women, if you are thirsty, ask any man for water. Men give the women water anytime they need, but don't waste it! Remember we have a long way ahead!"

Chapter

XXXVI

We all walked as a group behind the coyotes. The tall trees were endless along the way. We heard night animals everywhere. Our heavy steps made the loudest noise. No one said a word. We walked through the woods always aware of the noise of animals. It was after the first two hours that we began needing water. Mom, Sister, Auntie, and I used Alex's gallon to kill our thirst. After taking the first drink, our mouths started getting dry more often.

We stopped to rest before the sun came out, which was six hours after we had begun. Everything was going just fine. My burning eyes begged for sleep. That was when I started feeling the pain of my too-tight shoes. The discomfort in both feet was sharp. It became worse the longer I sat still.

People fell to sleep right away. I couldn't close my eyes even though I was very tired. I was aware of the sound of snakes which I began to hear in no time. The place was covered with trees. It was not the best place to be to avoid snakes, but it was a good place to hide from other types of danger.

People began snoring minutes after they closed their eyes. Although I couldn't see anything, I looked everywhere from my spot searching for poisonous animals. "Duermete!" Mom whispered as she laid next to me.

My eyes were closing, but my mind was wide awake. There was no way I could fall asleep peacefully in that place. My foot pain made everything worse. It was making my entire body feel pain. "If you want to sleep, do it here," Auntie told my sister pointing to her lap.

"Don't worry, you all go to sleep, I will watch out for you girls!" Alex told us sitting against a tree wide awake.

All I wanted to do was keep walking to get out of that place. I knew that was all I needed to make my pain go away too. I didn't complain even though it was getting worse and worse. When the sun was completely out, the coyotes woke everyone up signaling it was time to continue.

Some asked for water, others for food, and others just wanted to sleep a little longer. We ate, drank, and rested long enough to walk for the rest of the day until the moon came out again. All we ate were canned beans. We were still hungry after eating, but we had to save some for the rest of our trip.

Mom's allergies were starting to come back, slowly but surely. It was about eight in the morning when we started getting ourselves ready to continue. The day was not a bit warmer. I had a hard time walking again. My legs were not responding, and my feet had a burning sensation. I walked next to Alex, who seemed sleepy. The grass got taller as we walked. The silence made us feel like we were far away from immigration.

As the hours passed by, Mom's allergies got even worse. She sneezed constantly. Her nose was red, and her eyes didn't stop tearing. Before three p.m. that day, Alex's water gallon was gone. Mom tried hard not to drink so much water, so she wouldn't get anyone else sick.

We drank water from other people's gallons as we kept heading north. Auntie walked quietly with her head down all the time. My sister walked up front with the coyotes, which surprised me. She looked full of energy and ready to complete the trip.

By the time the sun was setting again, we had come across my only beautiful memory of the trip. We got to see many deer up close. It was beautiful and exciting to see real deer for the first time. They stared at us with their big eyes as we walked in line past them. They seemed harmless. We all smiled when we saw them. Everyone was amazed at their beauty. They were all over the place. It was scary for a second, but I saw them run away as we got close to them. They made me enjoy the trip for a few minutes.

As we moved away from them, people started begging for a break. We were all tired. We had walked for over nine hours, nonstop. The coyotes noticed Mom being very weak and said: "Let's get to those trees. We can rest there."

We took a few steps when we heard a helicopter fly near us. "Everyone down!" the coyotes yelled quickly. We all froze and threw ourselves down right where we were. We hoped the tall grass would protect us.

"God, please close their eyes!" I prayed silently.

I put my head down and froze like a statue to avoid calling the helicopter's attention. We all held our positions while it wandered around. No one moved. I was afraid even to breathe.

"Don't move! We already saw you!" a voice said through a speaker on the helicopter.

His words were like knives stabbing my heart. I listened without looking up. "Dios Mio!" a woman next to me cried from her place.

"Not again! What did I do wrong?" I lamented quietly.

"Pretend you are dead!" the coyotes advised without getting up from their place.

"Don't move!" the voice said through the speaker again. "Stop, stop!" he called over the speaker. I turned my head slowly trying to see exactly where the helicopter was located. "Freeze!" he yelled again.

I was very sure somebody was trying to run away. As I turned my head to look up, I was reminded of how amazing my Lord is. They were chasing three deer who were meters away from us. They ran quickly as the helicopter chased them from the air.

"Stop!" the man called again angrily as he flew away following them. We all started laughing as we saw them chase the beautiful animals. Wiping off our tears, we stood up and continued our path forward.

Chapter

XXXVII

*P*eople were almost crawling by the time we reached our resting area. It was surrounded by huge trees. As we sat down, the coyotes were planning on walking all night and sleep during the day, so we could see what us was around. Everyone agreed. They thought it was much safer for us to sleep while the sun was up.

Once again, we all ate for the second and last time of the day. Same menu: beans and water. My stomach was getting upset. I felt like throwing up for some reason. I wasn't hungry at all and I was beginning to feel dizzy.

My feet were hurting more than ever. Sitting in a spot away from Mom, I decided to take off my shoes for a little bit. My feet felt so swollen, and it was getting very hard to take them off. I felt weaker as my pain increased. After a painful try to get one of my shoes off, I saw why my feet hurt so much. My foot was covered in blisters. Not only that, but it was also bleeding from the same thing. The blood had dried, and my sock was stuck to my foot.

I didn't even try taking the socks off. It just seemed too painful. My dilemma was how to put my shoe back on. Only I noticed the condition of my foot. I fell asleep with my shoe off. People's stomachs cried from hunger. The beans were not enough to keep everyone full. The sound of the animals was around even during the day.

Time passed quickly while we rested. The day became night again, and everyone started getting ready as the moon came out. My legs were so weak that it was difficult to stand up again. People stood up even though they didn't feel ready to continue and so our second night of the trip began.

We were down to 10 gallons of water and 3 cans of beans when we started walking that evening. We didn't know exactly how far away we were from our destination. The coyotes told us we were close, and that the food and water would be enough. The pathway started looking different as we continued walking. There were fewer and fewer trees as we made our way forward until finally we came across empty land.

Many immigrants walked up front with the coyotes in a horizontal line, including Mom. The dim moon made the night more difficult. The light was not enough to see everything that was around us. As we moved for the first three hours, Mom was the first person to get thrown to the ground.

A huge wire wall of about 5-meters tall appeared in our path. It was nearly invisible. We could only feel it. Lots of people crashed against it hurting themselves in their faces.

The coyotes were surprised. According to them, it was the first time they had encountered the wire. We were all confused and fearful. Without thinking too much, we proceeded to climb the wire to get to the other side. It was not as easy as we thought. The hardest part was coming back down. The top of the wire was covered with pointy, sticky barbed wired that penetrated our skin easily.

Thinking it could be a trap, we got out of there as quickly as we could and continued our way. We didn't walk too far when we came across a second one. It was as tall as the first one. The big barbed wires tore people's clothes easily. The tall wires kept coming as we continued walking.

We came across at least thirty-five wires in three hours. That was more than enough to leave people tired, hurt, and bleeding. I saw people fall from the top of the wire to the ground. It was difficult for them to walk after that especially for older people.

We stopped when we saw the coyotes stand in place. They mumbled and looked at each other. It didn't take me too long to discern from their looks what I had been suspecting since we hit those wires: we were lost!

People stood there impatiently as the coyotes figured out what to do. They shook their heads and mumbled angrily about the coyotes. I had a feeling this would happen. We had no guidance other than the coyote's memory. It took them a while to agree on which way to go. No one had a clue where we were. We followed them hoping and praying they were taking us the right way.

I lost all track of time. All I knew was that it was still dark. People became weaker and felt increasingly hopeless as we moved in what we thought was a northern direction. Mom's allergies were getting worse, and the people carrying the few gallons of water that were left refused to share.

It was our second night in the forest, and we were not sure which way to go. We were surrounded by trees again. We forced our weak legs to keep moving. Mom, Sister, Auntie, and Alex walked up front right behind the coyotes. I slowly moved to the end of the line for two reasons:

1. Because it was getting so hard to keep up with them.
2. Because the people carrying the gallons of water were at the end.

I was hoping they would give me a sip of water if I carried the gallons or their personal stuff. I walked slowly next to one of the men carrying a gallon, keeping his pace and waiting for the right moment to ask for it. Suddenly, a bright light appeared right behind me. It went off so fast that I couldn't see anything.

"La migra! Corran!" the coyotes hollered from the very front. Everything happened so quickly that in a blink, everyone was gone. I stood there trying to see where my mother was, but she was gone as well. The last person I saw was the man carrying the gallon of water. I saw him hide behind the closest set of trees. I didn't know him, but I followed him hoping I would be safe. As he ran, I saw him throw the gallon of water. I was so thirsty that I went after it forgetting everything else.

The gallon had landed in the middle of small trees which had thorns all over the place. I came out of there with my face, arms and legs bleeding but with the gallon of water in my hands.

As I got up, I noticed the mistake I had made by going after the water. The last man was gone. And there I was, my eleven-year-old self, lost and alone in the forest in the middle of the night.

My body felt like a car running out of gasoline.

Knowing that immigration could be around, I hid behind a huge tree and sat there, drinking water. My heart was peaceful, but my mind was full of thoughts and fear. I started praying when I heard the sound of snakes around me. I was aware of the danger I was exposed to, but somehow my heart still felt calm.

I stood up after several minutes and saw no one around. I wandered around in circles looking for a way out, but all I saw were trees. Among the sea of trees, one of them captured my attention. It was about a half a mile from where I was standing. I had a feeling that it was the perfect place for me to hide. It didn't look any different from the rest, but I followed my feeling and walked toward that tree.

With the gallon of water still in my hands, I wiped some blood off my face and clenched my foot strongly to avoid feeling so much pain.

As I got to the tree, I walked deeper into it making as little noise as possible. Something made me stop. I heard noises that I was not making and as I continued walking, I saw two bright eyes scarily staring at me. It was so dark that I could see nothing else besides those eyes. I was sure it was some kind of wild animal.

My little heart accelerated as I moved closer. Suddenly, those sparkly, hazel eyes became familiar. "Mama?" I said pausing. I had found my mother. I was reunited with my mother and my sister under that tree who were the only two people there.

Chapter

XXXVIII

"*Mama, ya no puedo seguir!*" I finally confessed to her. "*Vamos a rendirnos mama, hay que encontrar a migracion para que nos lleven de regreso a casa!*" my sister begged. I was feeling so down. It didn't make any sense for us to continue if we were alone and lost.

"Girls, let's give them twenty minutes. If they don't come back to look for us, I promise we will find the border patrol and turn ourselves in!" Mom said.

I was so sure they were not coming back. I wanted to think they had gone without us, but that was not the case. It took them about twenty minutes to find us.

"*Que Bueno que las encontre!*" the coyote said as we came out of the trees. "*Ya estan todos reunidos, solo faltan ustedes!*" The people, especially the men, seemed very bothered.

"You should've leave them behind!" they argued as they saw us coming back. Their words made us angry, but we were in no condition to fight. Auntie and Alex mumbled angrily against them as they began to tell us the mean ideas the others had given the coyotes about us.

I was more disappointed about the fact that they had found us than I was about people's comments. There was still a long way to go, and I couldn't walk right. I swung from one way to another trying to keep up with the rest of the people.

My sight was becoming blurry. I was too tired, and so were most of the people. There was no way the coyotes would stop and rest near the spot we had seen the light. We had to continue until we were far enough away from that spot.

We walked that whole night still without a clue if we were heading the right way. We dropped our bodies to the ground and rested early in the morning. The gallon of water I had picked up didn't have a drop left after I shared it with some of the people.

I fell deeply asleep that morning. I didn't pay attention to what was around me this time. I could still hear the snakes, but I had no energy to even keep watching for them.

Mom, Sister, Alex, and Auntie laid beside me all sleeping like rocks. One of the coyotes wandered around while we slept. They were trying to figure out how to get on the right path again. Their cell phone had no signal, which made it even harder to get help and guidance. I can't begin to ponder all the things they did to figure out which way to go. However, when I woke up, they knew exactly where to go.

People celebrated with smiles once we were back on track. We took a long rest that lasted until the afternoon, and when the coyotes instructed us to do so, we stood up ready to continue. It was our second day in the forest, and we were about to hit the third night. Now that we knew which way to go, the coyotes were more patient with us. They knew we were tired, hungry, and thirsty. They didn't hassle us and allowed us to rest when most of the people felt tired.

The cold wind was getting stronger as we walked north. The temperature change was a good sign. We had no water or food left. We walked with our mouths completely shut to avoid getting thirsty. The day was over very quickly, and we found ourselves walking in the dark once again. The coyotes filled us with hope as we walked. Their phone began picking up signal which meant we were getting there. Our pain felt so worth it every time that phone had a bar of signal.

I wanted to crawl the rest of the way. My legs were weak as were everyone else's. We took a break of about one hour and then walked all night. Around five in the morning, we heard cars driving on the road. Our plan was to get to the road before the sun came out. The phone had enough signal to make the necessary call. We hit the road on time. The road was surrounded by grass on both sides, which was tall enough to keep us hidden from passing cars.

Luckily, there were not very many cars on that road. We listened carefully as we laid on the ground attentive to the next step. "There are three vans coming. They will park right on the side of the road. I want you all to jump to them very quickly. It does not matter which one you go in, they are all going to the same place" the coyote instructed.

We all ran to the white vans parked on the road quickly as the coyotes hassled us. I didn't even have time to ponder about how they would fit seventy people in only three vans. I realized what their plan was when they closed the doors. They laid us one on top of the other.

Unluckily, I was one of the first people to get in the van. A young man of about 200 pounds laid on top of me. I couldn't move. Neither could my mother, who was in the same van carrying another man on top. We were not allowed even to lift our heads. People began getting pissed as they noticed the coyotes relaxing in the front seats.

There was clearly room in the seats for a few more people, but they refused to let them sit there. The man on top of me felt so bad as he noticed me trying to stretch. He knew he was heavy, and he wanted to do something to help me.

We had been riding in that same van for a little less than an hour when I started running out of breath. There were still about two hours left to drive. People started telling the coyotes we couldn't breathe. "There is a little girl under me!" the man told them.

The coyotes didn't even bother to turn back to look. The immigrants started raising their voices one by one trying to get attention from the coyotes. Convinced that the coyotes wouldn't listen, one of the men lifted his head up, sat down and began screaming to them. "That's it! You have reached my limit!" he said.

"You will move some of us to another car, or I will make immigration come to us!" he threatened as he punched the van's windows.

"Get down and shut your mouth!" the Coyote yelled furiously.

"I didn't pay all this money to be treated like this!" the immigrant complained raising his voice even louder. He was hitting the windows so hard that I believed he would break them.

"Stop it! You will make the police notice us!" another coyote yelled angrily. "Get down!" they told him once again.

"I am not getting down unless you guys transfer us to another vehicle right now!" he demanded.

Half of the immigrants yelled with him supporting his idea. "Sir, please! Just calm down, we will be okay. Border patrol is going to catch us, and we are already on this side of the border! Think about all we went through these last couple of days. Please, do it for my daughters and lay down!" Mom begged. "No worries ma'am, this is my fifth time crossing the border, and I am very confident we are out of trouble at this point. The Coyotes are selfish, and we deserve a more comfortable place for the price we paid!" he argued.

He hit the windows harder and harder. "Transfer me to another vehicle!" he yelled. The traffic was completely stopped, and the noise had already captured some of the people's attention around the van. It was very surprising to see the coyotes solve the problem in less than 5 minutes. One of them had gotten out of the car and walked toward the closest truck in the middle of traffic. After exchanging a few words, they started moving people to that truck and two others.

The trip felt so much better after that movement. Unfortunately, Mom had a big bruise on her leg from having so much weight on top of her. One of her pants buttons came undone and was stuck to her leg. Just looking at it, hurt me so much.

After those two additional hours of driving, we made it safely and soundly to the house in Houston, Texas from where they would be delivering the people to their destinations. My sister came out of the last truck with only one shoe. She had lost the other one when the exchange of cars happened. It was somewhere in the middle of the road.

All the immigrants were amazed by the beauty of the house to which we were taken. It was a two-story, fancy, white house. The seventy immigrants were separated into groups and put in separate rooms. We all celebrated and made fun of each other as we took turns showering. Everyone smiled, enjoying the fact that we were officially in the United States of America.

It was not until my turn to shower came that everyone noticed my foot. My socks were completely covered in blood. People lamented that the youngest person in the entire group had suffered the most pain.

Mom didn't say a word; she didn't have to. Her expression told me everything she was thinking and feeling. Alex hugged me tightly saying: "If I could have changed something, I would have asked God to let me feel your pain instead." I smiled. That was about all I could do. The owners of the house gifted my sister and me a pair of slippers each. They joked with my sister saying, "Whoever finds your shoe in the middle of the road, is the guy you will marry when you grow up!"

It was so exciting to know we would see Dad in just a couple of hours, but it was bittersweet to say goodbye to the people who had come with us on that trip, as they left one by one.

The hardest person to say goodbye to was Alex. That night at the house in Houston was the last time we saw him. I wish I could find him and thank him for the attention and help he provided us. There was no one waiting for him on this side of the river. He had the difficult homework to begin a new life in this country by himself. "You are my family" he told us crying before we boarded my cousin's truck which would take us Dallas.

It was around 3am when we made it to Dad's arms that Tuesday beginning of February. People were lining up ready to welcome us. Everyone cried hardly in the dark patio of the apartment complex. Dad gave us the longest hugs ever as he cried along thanking God and apologizing to us for all we had to go through.

We still could not believe we were reunited once again. No words came out of my mouth. I didn't know what to say. All I wanted to do is keep hugging him and hear that we will never cross the border ever again.

Chapter

XXXIX

rossing the border illegally was not quite the hardest thing about coming to the United States. That was barely the beginning of all. Everything is so different here. Food, people, rules, school, and of course; the language. I remember my excitement when I saw the school I would attend for the first time. It was so different from the one in Mexico. My new middle school was huge! It was a two-story school with over 100 classrooms, a cafeteria, and separate fields for baseball, soccer, basketball, and track.

They offered choir, karate, soccer, music, and computer classes to mention only a few. We had none of those in Mexico. My first day of school caused a mixture of feelings. It had always been hard to express myself, and I knew that might be an issue. For the first couple of weeks, my parents advised us not to tell anyone that we had crossed the border illegally because we never knew how people would react to that.

It took me more than a couple of weeks to convince myself that I was already safe and sound living with Dad. It was like a trauma. I would close my eyes at night and wake up ten minutes later thinking I was sleeping in the middle of a forest.

Any sound I heard sounded like one I'd heard in the forest. I could still hear the animals and feel the cold air of the winter. It took a while for my feet to heal completely. I had to wear open shoes for the first couple days of school, which was the first reason that kids began to bully me.

They called me "Indian," "Big foot," and "Useless," while adding that I did not speak their language. ESL classes were the only classes I really enjoyed in school. I loved learning, and my ESL teachers were so much fun.

I did not feel any different when I was there. We were all the same, and none of the students in that class spoke any English. However, I was afraid of the rest of my classes. Being bullied every day was tough. I did not have any friends, and it was difficult trying to talk to people. The saddest part was that the people bullying me were Hispanics, just like me.

I didn't look up in classes that were not ESL. One of my Mexican classmates in my History class had put a desk at the very back of the room away from everyone else and demanded that I sit there because, according to him, I did not belong with them. The teacher had taken my classmate's action as an amicable gesture since there weren't any desks available.

It was a nightmare having to sit there every day as he threw things at me and reminded me that I did not belong. None of my other classmates did a thing to help me. I could feel the teacher was very nice. She smiled at me and made me feel welcome, unlike the students. I didn't complain to anyone because I was afraid it could get worse.

I had a huge thread in my throat when I went to those classes. I couldn't understand a thing, and I felt less and less valuable as the days passed. It was very hard to keep all that to myself. I couldn't understand what was so beautiful about this country anymore. I had gone through hell as I crossed the border and now everything seemed even worse.

I cried silently more than once during class hoping no one would see me and find one more reason to make fun of me. I felt like I had no right to defend myself. Everyone I turned to was much better than me in every way including the people who bullied me.

My sister was having the same problems. We both went home crying constantly and implored Mom with broken hearts to get us out of school. "I will work if you want, but I do not want to go back to school ever again," we told her.

She didn't know why. Neither one of us told her because our fear was stronger than anything else. Mom would cry next to us saying: "I will not take away the opportunity to become what you dream of becoming. I prefer you to hate me now instead of hating your own future."

She was tough on us, but she went to school to talk to the principals and some teachers about what was going on. My sister and I denied everything when they asked us if we were afraid of something or someone.

She and I were doing great in our ESL classes. We always had the highest grades in the class. We really wanted to learn so people would stop bullying us.

At the end of our first school year in the United States, our teachers rewarded us with about five honor rolls which were given to us in front of the entire school. I was neither happy nor proud of myself. The honor rolls meant nothing to me since I couldn't speak any English. Instead, I felt embarrassed. No matter how good my ESL teachers spoke about me, I did not believe a word they said.

Chapter

XL

 uring our second school year, my sister and I were separated. She was now in high school, and I was finishing my last year in middle school. It was our first full school year in the US.

My sister and I didn't really talk much about school, but we knew from each other's faces that we were still going through hell.

I felt even more unprotected not having my sister around during school. Besides the ESL kids, it was very hard to make friends with other people.

As time passed, my teachers realized how much I cared about school and appreciated the efforts I was making. Some of them were kind enough to give me different work than the rest of my classmates. Of course, it was subject related but that way, they gave me an equal opportunity to make my grades go up without anyone helping me.

Other teachers took the time to create a Spanish copy of whatever we were reading every now and then and give it to me so I could join the class that way. It was a lot of extra work for them, and it meant the world to me. They began putting my heart back together and awakened my desire to keep learning.

For some reason, my fourth period was always my worst class every single year until I became a senior in High School.

During my first year of high school, I had an even rougher time. All ESL classes were removed from my schedule due to the good grades I was making in that subject. It was even harder to attend regular classes with kids who were either born in this country or brought to the US as babies; in other words, they spoke and understood English perfectly.

It was a beatdown trying to figure out what I was supposed to do during class. As I talked to some of my classmates, I noticed some of them had sadly forgotten their roots. They would deny they spoke Spanish and that they were Hispanics, I guess it was a good thing because they made me practice my English.

I learned to protect myself by explaining to my teachers in advance that I did not speak English. My high school teachers gave me a feeling of comfort after that. They assigned one of the kids from the class to translate when they needed to speak to me, and it was those translations of recognition and positive comments that made me understand how valuable I was.

As the days went by, I was able to understand more and more, until I began having higher grades than those who spoke perfect English. With that, I not only got the recognition from my teachers but most importantly the respect of those people who believed I had no future.

High school days went smoother as I began to have more faith and give myself some credit for what I was accomplishing day by day.

One day during my Sophomore year, my English teacher assigned an essay for an exam grade. The subject was: write about the hardest thing you had to go through so far in your life. It was then that I shared my story about crossing the border illegally for the first time with my teacher who I thought would be the only person reading it.

I took my time writing everything I felt during those days on that blank piece of paper. I went two pages over what the teacher asked for, and the next day as the class was beginning, Mr. Terry, with a broken voice asked me in front of the entire class if I could come up to the front and read my essay out loud.

I felt my face turn hot immediately. I felt my story was something very personal that I did not want to share with everyone, but I couldn't argue with my teacher, so I did it. Remembering everything as I read was not easy at all. My voice began to break, and I cried mid-sentence.

I could not hold my tears back no matter how hard I tried, and I never looked up while I was reading. Those were among the most awkward ten minutes of my life. I kept my head down when I finished avoiding people from seeing my red eyes.

There was complete silence when I finished reading. It made me wonder if they had even understood what I had read. "Please lift your head up and look around you," my teacher told me. I did as I was told, slowly, and noticed that the entire class was crying silently along with me.

They stood up and began applauding me without anyone telling them to do it. Two of my American classmates walked up to me and hugged me tightly after that. The applause didn't stop until I sat back down at my desk.

"You just touched forty souls with a four-page essay. Imagine what a full story could do if you share it with the world!" my teacher said finally.

I walked out of the classroom feeling more secure of myself. From that day forward, my teacher referred to me as "my novelist." He encouraged me throughout the entire year to write my story. I didn't take his words seriously; I didn't know I should.

As my Sophomore, Junior, and Senior year went by, I began sharing my story with more people and especially with those who I felt needed to hear it.

Mr. Terry didn't keep the story to himself; he shared it with my English teachers as the years passed. All of them asked me to narrate what I had gone through since they had no concept of such an experience. I enjoyed seeing them pay so much attention to my story and being so into it.

Every single one of them motivated and pushed me to write my full story on paper; until I finally listened to them.

Throughout these years, I've had ups and downs. It was hard having to "hide" being illegal in the US. It was even tougher to realize that we don't have equal rights no matter how good of a person or how much love you have for the country.

Chapter

XLI

*M*y years after graduating from high school didn't get any easier. I had to begin working in my sophomore year to help my family. My first job was as a janitorial worker. My family and I worked together cleaning houses, schools, and churches. We didn't get paid much since we worked for someone else. My aspirations to continue my education began to fade as I noticed my parents struggling to keep a roof over our heads.

It was then that I told myself I would work for a while to help my parents and then go back to school. However, my plans didn't work out that way. The money that all 4 of us made was just enough to cover our expenses. I was tired of seeing Mom and Dad work so much for the little money they made.

We all had no energy by the end of the week. We couldn't even have a meal together; as a family anymore. My sister worked all night and slept during the day. I worked all day and slept all night. My father had two jobs, and we barely saw him. The only time I saw my mother was when she slept.

There were days when I locked myself in the closet and cried silently, complaining to God about the type of life He was giving me. I was unhappy. I hated not being able to do the type of things that girls my age did. It was not fun. I felt different from them. I couldn't consider anyone my friend, and the couple girls I knew who were my age, talked about all the fun things they did.

I was angry. I wanted to yell out loud that I was tired of my life. Temptations were all around me. Many times, I thought of harming myself to see if anyone even cared about me anymore. My path kept getting tougher and tougher.

Two years after I graduated from High School, my mother made a decision that changed my life drastically. After several weeks of having no communication with Dad, they decided to separate. Not only that, but she decided to go back to Mexico to take care of my sick grandpa, who was on his last stage of life.

Even with all the pain in my heart, I had to admit that was the best decision. I was tired of watching them hurt each other not only mentally, but also physically. Their confrontations were getting worse and worse.

The abusive environment that I had seen since I was very little, beginning with grandma and grandpa, aunts, and uncles, and now Mom and Dad gave me a negative view of marriage.

I was convincing myself that I would never get married because I didn't want to have that type of life. I cried almost every night after my mother left. I felt empty.

Things got even worse a couple of months later when my sister decided to move in with her boyfriend because of my father's attitude. I hated my life. I couldn't find one positive thing about it. Then one day I turned on my radio, and these words spoke to me, "Imagine all the people living life in peace."

I knew that to make a change, I had to start with myself. I needed guidance, and I didn't have anyone at that moment to guide me. So, I decided for the very first time in my life to open an old bible that was in my father's closet. It was the best decision I ever made, and I only regretted not having done it before.

I noticed how interesting the Bible was even when I hated reading. It was as if the book was speaking to me as I continued.

I realized how wrong things can go when you don't find them out for yourself. It opened my eyes, and I learned that the teachings and beliefs I had been following were wrong. My faith was building as I turned the pages.

For the first time in a while, I felt peace even during the hard times I was going through. My scriptures made me see all the positive things in life. It made me understand the last golden advice my mother had given me before she left. She said: "Look in your mirrors and decide what you want for yourself."

It was then that I understood that my "mirrors" were all the people around me. I began to put myself in their shoes and see life from their places. Doing that helped me continue my path in a straight way. I recalled moments when people around me got drunk and crazy and saying to myself: "I do not want to be like them."

That motivated me to never touch alcohol, cigarettes, or drugs. I kept myself busy all the time to avoid having arguments with Dad. Slowly and secretly, I started investigating different churches and learning about different religions. I attended different churches with some of my friends, but none of them gave me the feeling I was looking for. Instead, they scared me with their screams and acts.

I trusted the Lord with all my heart and prayed to him for guidance until I came across the Church of Jesus Christ of Latter-Day Saints. The moment I learned about this church, I felt as if I had been a member my entire life. Without knowing it even existed, I was already following their rules and beliefs.

I was baptized a couple months later after investigating, reading, and praying about it for myself. The same feeling I had on the night I got lost in the forest by myself, took me to the waters of baptism. I saw over time how much the Gospel had changed me. It was sad seeing a whole lot of strangers at my baptism. I knew I could count on them all from that moment on, but there weren't any family or close friends with me on that special day.

I met some of the best people at church. They gave me the love, comfort, and motivation I was seeking. As the months went by, my father and my sister opened their hearts and followed me to the waters of baptism.

I cannot explain how much joy I had in life after that. I wanted everyone to feel the same way I did, so I began sharing the Gospel with close friends. I share my testimony knowing with all my heart that your prayers can be answered, and your life can find peace if you really believe and seek the truth.

I write all these things hoping that my story can motivate and inspire that one person out there for whom God made me write all this. Don't ever give up! If one day you feel like you are at a dead end, think about how boring life would be if we didn't have trials.

Imagine you and all the people in the world having all the money, power, and things you ever wished for. What would the rest of your life be like twenty years later when you have traveled everywhere and bought yourself everything you wanted? Who would you help if everyone had that style of life? Wouldn't a life without trials be tougher?

"When you are alone and don't know when the night will end just remember its never too long so be strong cause there's always a ray of hope".— David Archuleta (song "Aiming for Hope")

"Give me your tired, your poor,
Your huddled masses yearning to breathe free,
The wretched refuse of your teeming shore.
Send these, the homeless, tempest-tost to me,
I lift my lamp beside the golden door!" – Emma Lazarus

CPSIA information can be obtained
at www.ICGtesting.com
Printed in the USA
LVHW021027041119
636238LV00003B/390